▶▶ *FastForward*™

RockSolid Drum Patterns

with Dave Zubraski

Wise Publications
London / New York / Sydney / Paris / Copenhagen / Madrid

Exclusive Distributors:
Music Sales Limited
14-15 Berners Street, London W1T 3LJ, UK.
Music Sales Pty Limited
20 Resolution Drive, Caringbah, NSW 2229, Australia.
Music Sales Corporation
257 Park Avenue South, New york, NY10010,
United States of America.

Order No. AM92666
ISBN 0-7119-4799-6
This book © Copyright 1997 by Wise Publications.

Book design by Michael Bell Design.
Edited and arranged by Dave Zubraski.
Music processed by Seton Music Graphics.
Cover photography by George Taylor.
Cover instrument kindly loaned by
The Bass & Drum Cellar.
Text photographs courtesy of
London Features International.
Printed and bound in the United Kingdom.

Your Guarantee of Quality:
As publishers, we strive to produce every book to
the highest commercial standards.
The music has been freshly engraved and the book has
been carefully designed to minimise awkward page turns
and to make playing from it a real pleasure.
Particular care has been given to specifying acid-free,
neutral-sized paper made from pulps which have not
been elemental chlorine bleached.
This pulp is from farmed sustainable forests and
was produced with special regard for the environment.
Throughout, the printing and binding have
been planned to ensure a sturdy, attractive publication
which should give years of enjoyment.
If your copy fails to meet our high standards, please
inform us and we will gladly replace it.

www.musicsales.com

Introduction

The foundation of any rock band is the rhythm section, which is formed by the bass and drums. Together they must form a solid groove for the other members to play and sing over.

No matter how good the individual musicians may be, the band will only be as good as the rhythm section allows.

This book sets out to give you a selection of usable rock rhythms and fills, along with some ideas of how to expand and adapt them to create your own style.

Each example is demonstrated on an accompanying audio track with a band, so you will develop an understanding of how to use each rhythm and fill when playing with your own band.

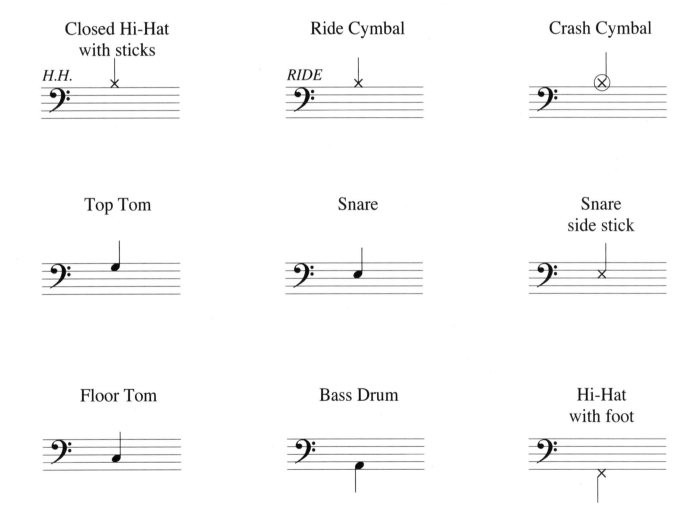

All the examples in this book have been written assuming you are right handed.

However, if you are left handed, play all examples with reverse hands and feet.

Basic Rock Rhythms With Variations

To become a good rock drummer there are
three basic points to remember when practising
the examples in this book.

1. Keeping Good Time

This means not speeding up or slowing down
during a song. To help you develop a good sense
of time, practise all the examples with the audio
tracks and with a metronome.

Try playing each example at different tempos,
from slow through to fast. Say the count (which
is written above the notes) aloud.

2. Playing With A Solid Feel

Don't be afraid to hit the drums. This is not
to say you have to 'bash' them, but to obtain the
right feel and sound from your kit, you have to
strike the drums and cymbals with enough power
to sound confident and solid while being relaxed
at the same time.

If you feel yourself getting tense at any time,
stop and take a short break before continuing.

3. Playing With Originality

Having mastered each of these examples try
experimenting and adapting them to let your
own personality come through.

Each example has two corresponding audio
tracks. The first track is rhyth a full rock band
which demonstrates how to use each rhythm
and fill.

The second audio track has the band minus
drums giving you the opportunity to take the
driving seat and play along.

Each example starts with a four-beat count.

So let's start with Example 1: this is a very
basic rock rhythm in $\frac{4}{4}$ which (when played with
a good feel) works so well because it provides an
uncluttered, solid foundation, allowing the
rest of the band freedom to play over the top.

TRACKS 1+2 **EXAMPLE 1**

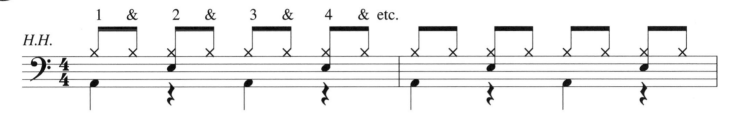

Now try playing the same rhythm but with
a variation.

Move the closed hi-hat pattern (which is
played with your right hand) onto the

floor-tom and play the snare part (which is
played with your left hand) onto the top-tom.

This gives the rhythm a much heavier feel.

TRACKS 3+4 **EXAMPLE 2**

In Example 3, we have another variation, this time we play a quarter note ride cymbal pattern (with your right hand) and add the hi-hat (played with your left foot) on beats 2 and 4 which are called the 'off' beats.

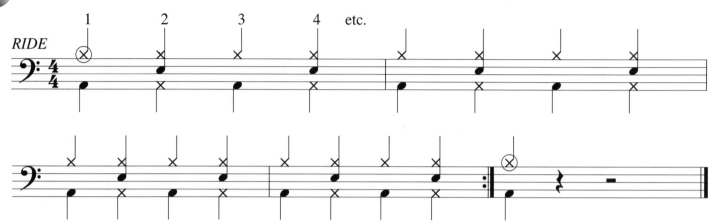

In Example 4, the snare beats are played using the side stick as shown in Photograph B (page 10). This produces a much lighter sound and feel to the rhythm.

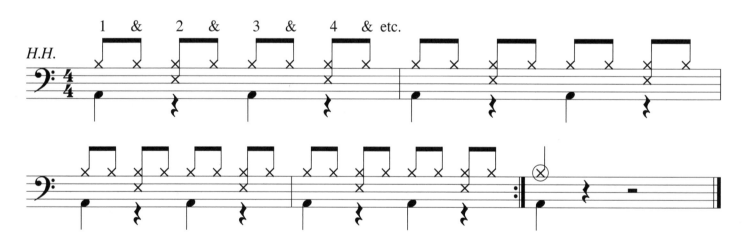

Having practised all the examples in this section separately, try playing them through from Examples 1 to 4 without stopping.

Play four or eight bars of each example and you will see how these simple variations can make the same basic rhythm sound very different without losing the groove.

When playing in a rock band it is important to use dynamics (i.e. the contrast between loud and soft) to make your music sound interesting as well as marking out the different sections of a song.

▶▶ **GINGER BAKER (CREAM)**

*"...drums are a very important part of all cultures.
The drum is something that all races have in common.
It's the most important instrument. Armies march to the drummer.
The drums, the drums... a drummer can influence the whole band.
You know the old saying: A good band with a bad drummer is a bad band.
But I know my drums, and I have studied basic harmony
and all this stuff because I thought it was important.
If the band ain't in tune, it don't swing..."*

When playing the snare drum there are three basic ways to strike the drum.

The first method is to strike the head near to the centre of the drum, letting the stick bounce back off the head with each beat played. This will produce a good clear note letting the full tone of the drum be heard.

The second way is to strike the drum head and the rim at the same time (as shown below).

This is called a rim shot and will produce a much louder note with a very hard tone.

The third is to lay the stick across the drum, and with your left hand (in the centre) laying on top, hold the stick between your thumb and first finger, leaving your other fingers resting lightly on the head.

Different sounds will be obtained depending on which part of the stick hits the rim so try experimenting. Usually the butt end is in contact with the rim as shown below. This is called a side stick.

In Example 5, we play the basic rock rhythm as practised in Chapter 1 and use the variations to give dynamics to this piece of music.

Note: In audio example 10 the drums come in after the four beat count.

Rock Rhythms With Bass Drum Variations

As I said in the introduction, it is important for the drummer to form a solid groove with the bass player. In order to achieve this your bass drum pattern should closely follow the notes being played by the bass guitar, or vice-versa.

In Example 6, we have a good example of bass and drums working together. Listen to how the bass drum pattern locks in with the bass guitar.

TRACKS 11+12 EXAMPLE 6

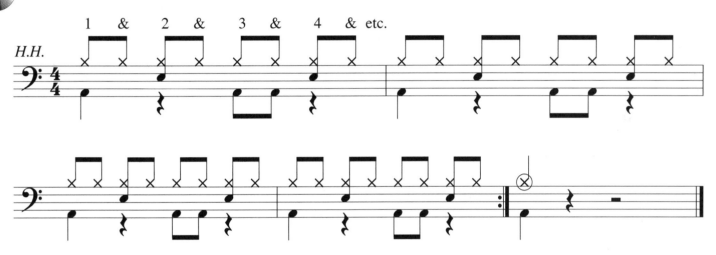

In Example 7, we have a different bass drum pattern. When playing these rhythms make sure each bass drum beat falls exactly in time with the hi-hat pattern.

TRACKS 13+14 EXAMPLE 7

13

Try experimenting with different bass drum
foot positions to find which works best for you.

For example, play with your foot flat on the
pedal and then try playing with your heel raised.

The height at which you sit will also affect
your playing so, again, experiment; try different
stool positions until you feel comfortable and
in control of the pedal.

TRACKS 15+16 EXAMPLE 8

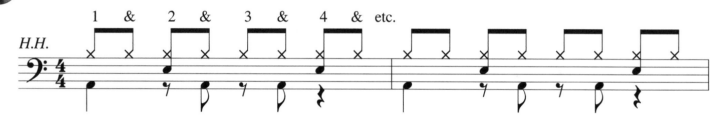

Next we have two more simple but effective
bass drum patterns. When locked in with the
bass guitar they make for rock solid grooves.

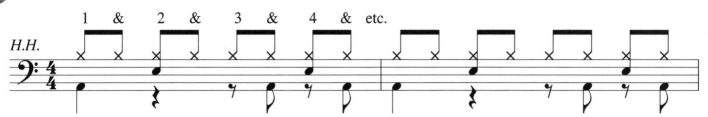

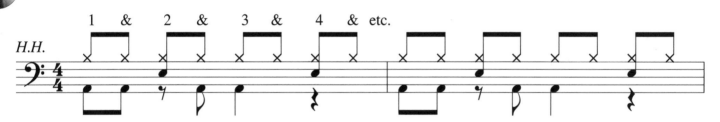

When you are confident you can play these
bass drum rhythms as written, try experimenting
with them.

For example, play the closed hi-hat pattern on
the floor-tom or ride cymbal etc.

▶▶ **LARRY MULLEN JR. (U2)**
"I started off... doing military drumming and from there, I had this style of having to fill in... When the band formed, they thought I was great because I was able to fill in. But as it developed, they started to say "try not to put so many rolls in" - and it's only lately that I've managed to cut back. I used to be able to do drum solos - but I can't anymore..."

Rock Rhythms With Snare Drum Variations

Now let's look at rhythms involving different snare drum patterns.

In Example 11 the snare falls on beat 2 and on the '&' after beats 3 and 4 (except in bars 4 and 8).

Make sure the snare beats fall exactly in time with the closed hi-hat pattern, or your playing will sound sloppy.

 **TRACKS 21+22** **EXAMPLE 11**

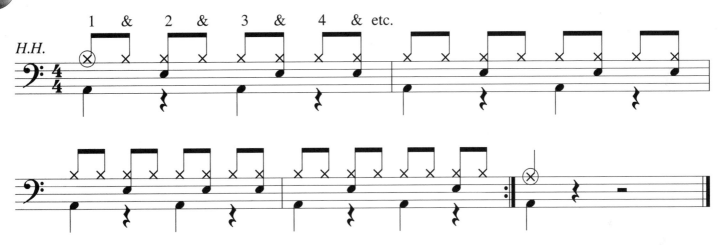

In Example 12 the snare falls together with the closed hi-hat on every '&' beat.

TRACKS 23+24 **EXAMPLE 12**

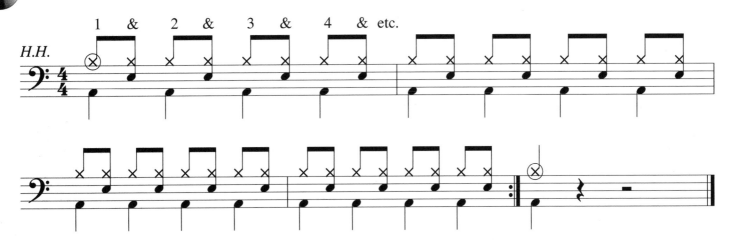

In the next example the snare plays a quarter note pattern, producing a hard driving rhythm.

TRACKS 25+26 **EXAMPLE 13**

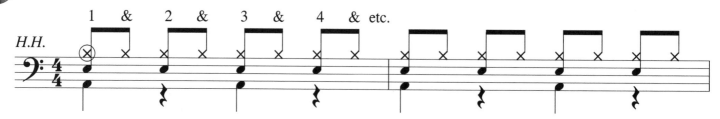

When playing these rhythms, try using different amounts of pressure (with your left foot) to keep the hi-hat pedal closed.

You will find when more pressure is applied to the pedal you will get a tighter sound.

Less pressure will result in a looser, heavier sound.

Again you can apply this technique to get more colour and variety into your playing.

In Example 14, the snare falls on beat 3, opening up the rhythm and giving a half-time feel to this groove.

TRACKS 27+28 **EXAMPLE 14**

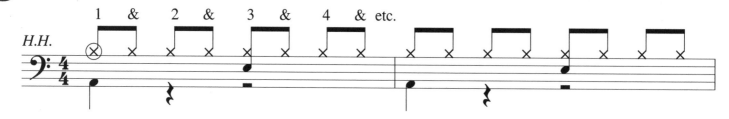

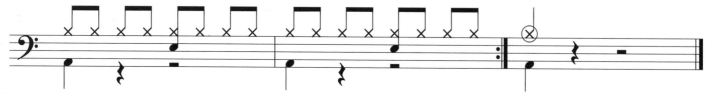

▶▶ *CHARLIE WATTS (THE ROLLING STONES)*

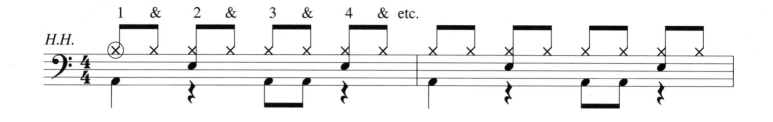

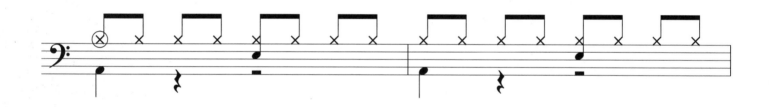

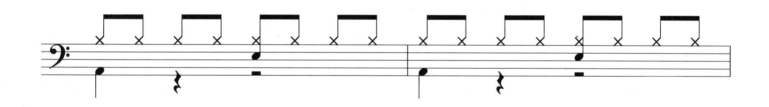

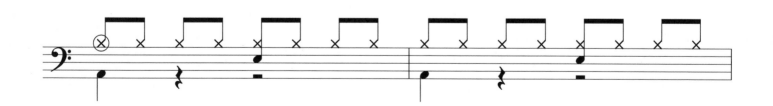

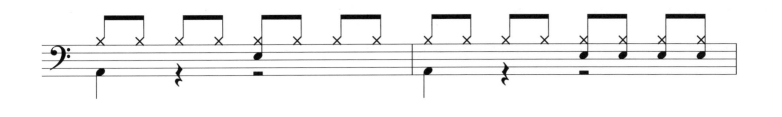

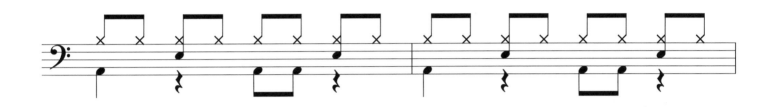

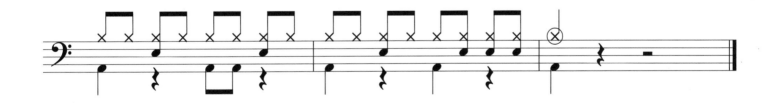

Different Bass And Snare Drum Patterns

So far we have looked at rhythms using different bass and snare drum patterns in separate examples, but in this section we will combine these ideas to form more interesting rhythms.

By using this kind of 'mix & match' approach to your drumming you vastly increase the number of subtly different patterns available to you.

Again, don't be afraid to experiment.

Example 16 combines the bass drum pattern from Example 10 with the snare pattern from Example 11.

When you play these examples for the first time, try breaking them down by playing the hi-hat and bass drum part first, then the hi-hat and snare drum part, finally bring both of them together to form the complete example.

 **TRACKS 31+32 EXAMPLE 16**

Don't forget, it's important to practise all the examples in this book at different tempos.

A drummer must be able to sound confident playing at slow tempos as well as fast.

TRACKS 33+34 **EXAMPLE 17**

In Example 18, the snare falls on beat 4, giving this rhythm an interesting half-time feel.

TRACKS 35+36 **EXAMPLE 18**

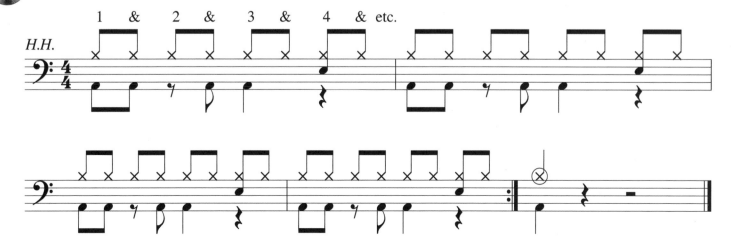

Having practised all these rhythms as written,
try playing the closed hi-hat pattern on the
ride cymbal and add the hi-hat (played with
your left foot) on beats 2 and 4.

 **TRACKS 37+38** EXAMPLE 19

In Example 20, we combine a quarter note snare
pattern with an eighth note bass drum pattern.

 **TRACKS 39+40** EXAMPLE 20

Drum Fills

Drum fills are generally used when moving from one section of a song to another.

When you play a drum fill it is important to keep the tempo and groove rock steady.

Often a simple but effective one or two beat fill will flow better than one over a whole bar or more. There is nothing worse than a busy drummer getting in the way of a good song, playing fills that trip up not only you, but the whole rhythm section.

In this section, we have six different fills starting on different beats of the bar. The music has been written in four-bar sections so the fills are played in every fourth bar.

Note the cymbal pattern changes from the closed hi-hat to the ride (or vice versa) after every fill.

In Example 21, we have a half beat fill starting on the '&' of beat 4.

Note: The suggested sticking written above the fill: R = right hand, L = left hand.

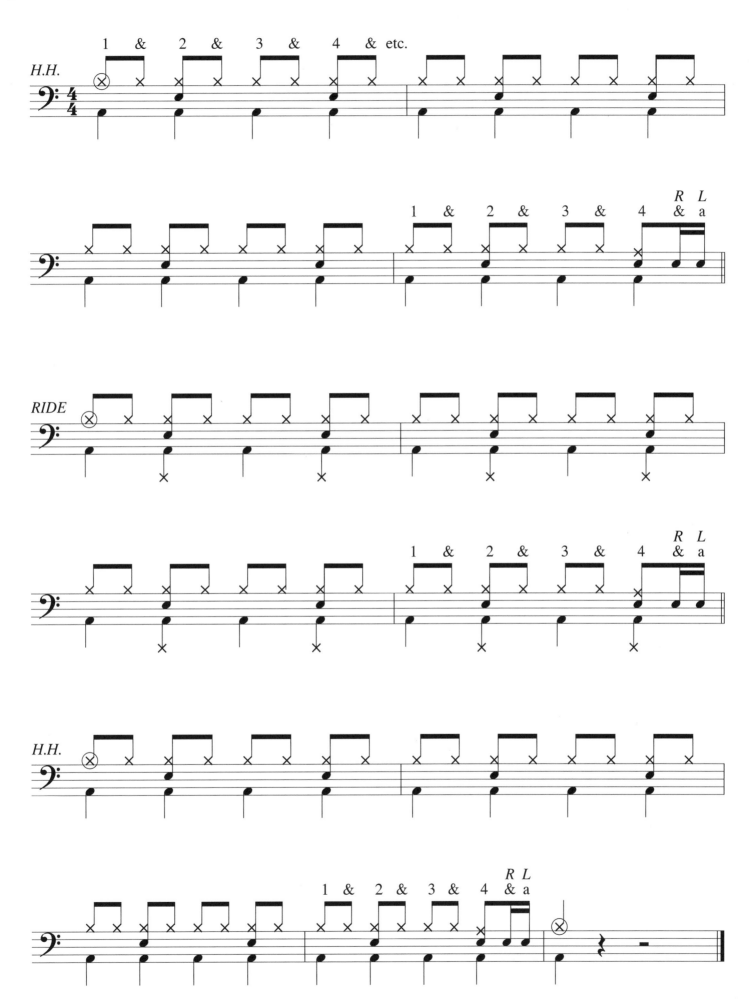

In Example 22, we have a one-beat fill
starting on beat 4. These very short fills can
be very effective.

 TRACKS 43+44 EXAMPLE 22

In Example 23, the fill starts on the '&' after
beat 3.

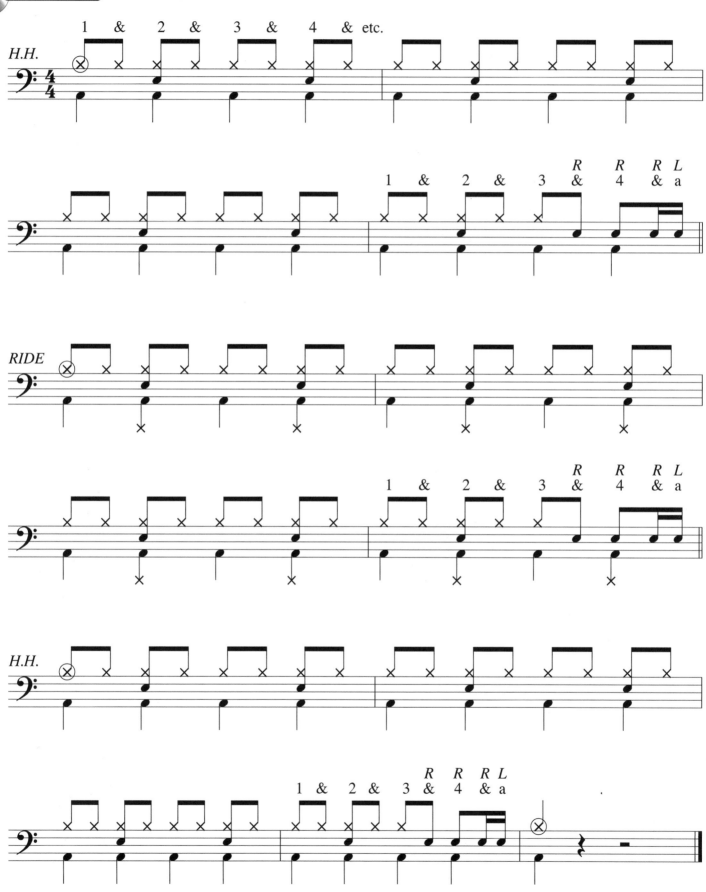

In Example 24 we have another fill starting on the '&' after beat 3, though this one is busier, with its repeated sixteenth notes.

Note: All these fills will work with any of the rhythms from the previous chapters.

In Example 25, we have a two-beat fill starting on beat 3.

As you will have guessed by now, these fills are working their way back through the last bar of each pattern, getting progressively more complex.

▶▶ *FastForward*™
Guide To Drums

Crash Cymbal

Top-Tom

Cymbal Stand

Ride Cymbal

Hi-Hat Cymbals

Cymbal Stand

Snare Drum

Floor Tom

Hi-Hat Stand

Bass Drum

Bass Drum Pedal

Snare Drum Stand

Setting Up Your Kit

A basic kit comprises a bass (or 'kick') drum, snare, top tom-tom, floor tom, hi-hat stand, snare drum stand, bass drum pedal, two cymbal stands, one pair of hi-hat cymbals, one ride cymbal and one crash cymbal, as shown above.

Drums and cymbals come in a wide range of sizes but for Hip Hop I would recommend a kit comprising of the smaller sizes. This is because as opposed to the big, ambient rock sound, Hip Hop sounds tend to be tight, small, funky and off the wall. A possible set up would comprise of: 20" bass drum, 12" and 13" top-toms, 14" floor-tom and a 5"x14" metal snare drum with 13" hi-hat cymbals, 16" and 17" crashes and a 20" heavy ride cymbal.

When setting up your kit make sure everything is within easy reach. The height of your drum stool is important as this can affect the way you play. Go for a position where your legs are relaxed and in control of the pedals.

Tuning and the choice of drum heads can make a big difference to the overall sound of a drum.

The tighter you tune a drum the higher its pitch will become. This also affects the speed of the stick response. The tighter the head the faster the response.

When tuning the snare drum try to have both heads quite tight with the snares just taut enough to stop them from rattling. If the snares are too tight it can stop them vibrating freely, causing them to sound choked.

Choose a head that is not too heavy as this can dull the sensitivity of the snares. I would suggest you try a Remo CS (centre spot) head for the batter (top) side and a Remo Ambassador Snare for the snare head (bottom side).

Tom-toms are not usually tuned to any specific notes but the smaller sizes are tuned to a higher pitch, getting lower as the sizes get larger. One thing to keep in mind when tuning the toms is to make sure they all have the same decay time (the time it takes for the sound to die away).

Pull-Out Chart

The Bass Drum

The bass drum is generally tuned as low as possible without losing its tone. To achieve this tighten the heads only enough to take the wrinkles out. A pillow or blanket placed inside the drum against the back head is often used as damping to cut the ring down and produce a good solid thud.

There are two basic ways of playing the bass pedal. One way is to have the whole foot flat on the pedal, as shown in the first picture below. The other way is to raise the heel of your foot and only use your toes, as shown in the second picture.

Sometimes a combination of both methods is used. You might find using the toe method is easier for playing faster patterns. Try both ways to see which is the more comfortable for you.

When adjusting the tension spring on the bass pedal don't have it too tight or too loose. There should be just enough tension in the spring so that when you rest your foot on the pedal, the weight of your foot is enough to move the beater onto the head.

Bass drum beaters are usually made from felt or wood. A hard felt beater is the most commonly used as this produces a fast response and a good tone.

Care & Maintenance

Batter Head

Tension Rod
Lug

Snare Tension
Screw

Snare Counter
Hoop

Snares (not seen)

Snare Gate

Batter Counter Hoop

Tension Rod

Metal Shell

Snare Strainer
Control Lever

Snare Head
(not seen)

A few points on general care and maintenance. A well maintained kit will last longer, look better and, what is more, important, be less likely to let you down on a gig or recording session.

1) Keep all tension rods, screws, springs, snare release etc. lightly oiled.

2) As the snares are the most delicate part of the kit, try not to touch them unnecessarily and do not lay anything on top of them as this can cause the thin strands of wire to bend. If this happens the snares will vibrate unevenly causing an annoying buzz.

3) Cymbals can be cleaned (not too often) with a cymbal cleaner (obtained at most music stores) or washed with warm soapy water using a sponge, making sure you completely dry the cymbal after washing. Be careful not to use anything abrasive like metal cleaner or scouring pads as this can damage a cymbal. Do not clamp your cymbals to the stands too tightly as this can prevent them from vibrating freely and possibly cause them to crack.

4) Most drum heads are made of plastic and are very durable. However, with constant use they will gradually lose their tone and become less responsive and should be replaced.

To change a drum head, first unscrew (using a drum key) and remove all the tension rods, then lift off the counter hoop.

Remove the old head and fit the new one, replace the counter hoop and tension rods, then tune the head by tightening each tension rod in sequence (as shown in the diagram below) by one turn, until the required sound and feel are obtained.

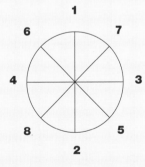

5) Do not store your drums too near a heat source e.g. radiator, open fire etc.

6) When transporting your kit a set of waterproof fibre cases is recommended. These come in all different sizes so make sure you know the measurements of your drums before buying them.

Holding The Sticks

There are two basic ways of holding the sticks. One way is the matched grip, where both sticks are held in the same way.

The other is the traditional grip. Most rock drummers favour the matched grip (for power and speed) as shown below.

Matched Grip

Right hand: With the palm of your right hand facing towards the floor, hold the stick about one third of the distance from the butt end, so it pivots between the ball of the thumb and the joint of the first finger, as shown in the photograph.

Let your first finger curl around the stick, then bring your second, third and fourth fingers gently around onto the stick to guide and stabilise it.

Left hand: The left hand grip should be exactly the same as the right hand. Try to keep both hands and fingers as relaxed as possible.

Now we've worked our way back to the '&' after beat 2. Note the fill used in this example goes from the snare to the top tom then down to the floor tom.

Note: Having played this fill using single stroke sticking, for example, R L R L *etc.*

Try playing it with double stroke sticking. For example, L L R R *etc.*

Syncopated Rock Rhythms

So far, in all the previous examples the snare
drum pattern has fallen in time with one or more
of the hi-hat beats. In this section we will look at
rhythms that have snare patterns falling with,
and between, the closed hi-hat beats. These are
called syncopated rhythms.

In Example 27, the sixteenth note syncopated
snare beat falls on the 'a' after beat 3.

When playing these examples make sure your
closed hi-hat plays a constant eighth note rhythm
and does not follow the snare pattern.

 **TRACKS 53+54** EXAMPLE 27

In Example 28, the sixteenth note syncopated
snare beat falls on the 'a' before beat 2.

TRACKS 55+56 EXAMPLE 28

In Example 29, we have a rhythm with two
syncopated snare drum beats.

TRACKS 57+58 EXAMPLE 29

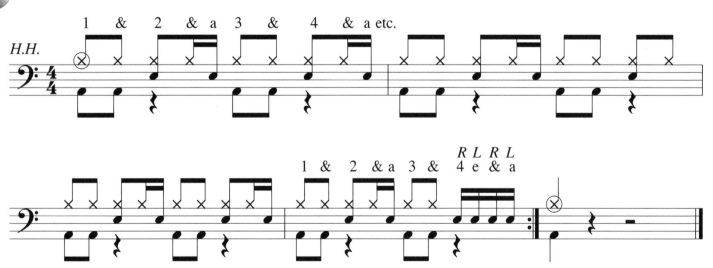

Syncopated rhythms tend to sound busier
than the previous examples we have covered,
so although they are exciting and fun to
play you have to be careful not to make the
music sound too cluttered by over-using them.

▶▶ *JOHN BONHAM (LED ZEPPELIN)*
"I think that feeling is a lot more important in drumming than technique.
It's all very well to be playing a triple paradiddle - but who's going to know if you're actually doing it.
If you pay too much attention to technique you sound like every other drummer does.

In Example 30, we have used a syncopated
rhythm to add dynamics to a piece of music.

A straight rock beat is played for the first eight
bars and then a more exciting syncopated rhythm
is played for the following eight bars.

These two sections are then repeated.

 **TRACKS 59+60** **EXAMPLE 30**

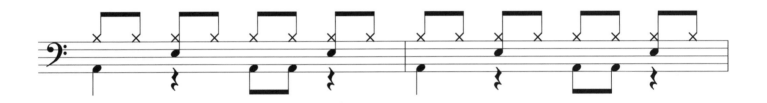

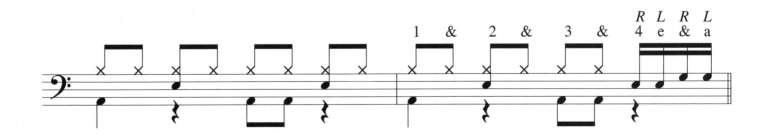

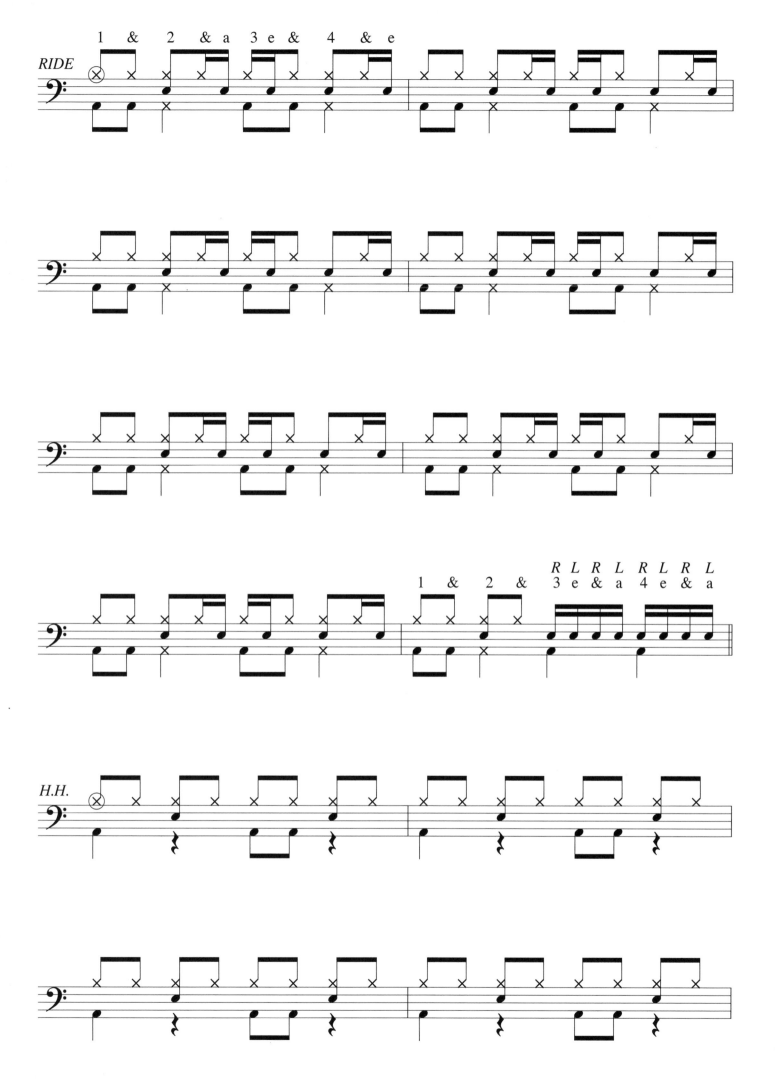

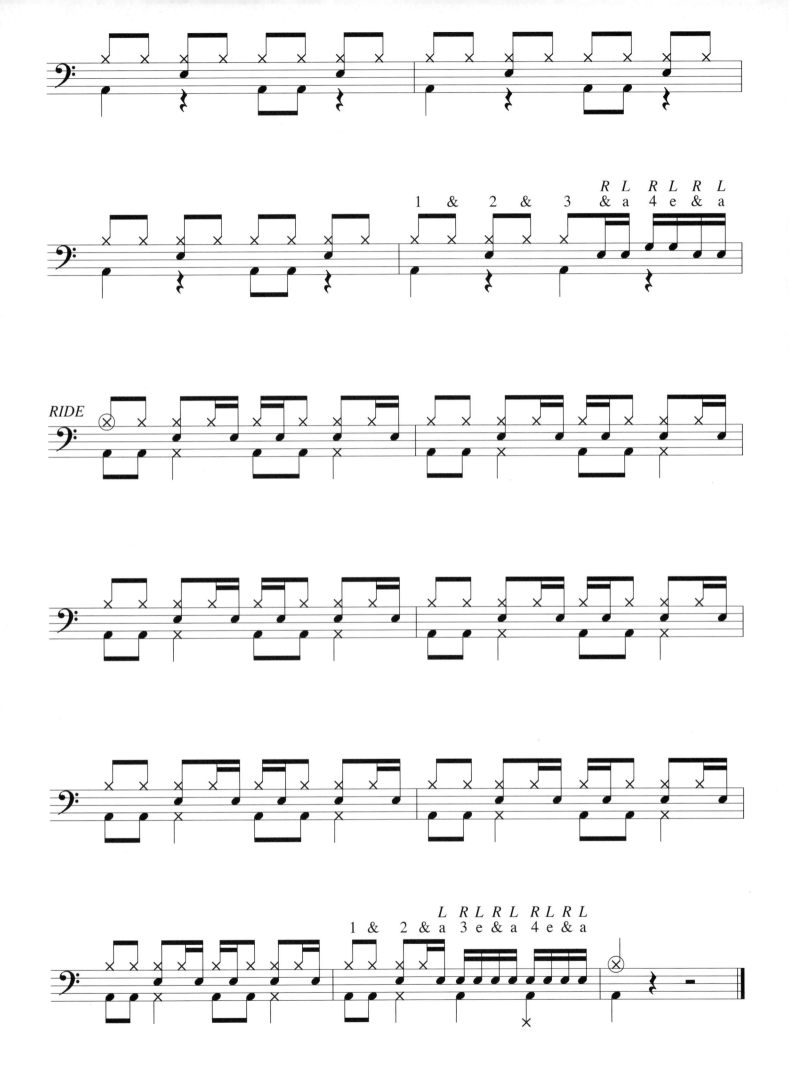

"We've done this band longer than school, longer than marriage, longer than anything."

Sixteenth Note Bass Drum Patterns

So far, in all the previous rhythms we have only used quarter and eighth note bass drum patterns. In this section we will look at rhythms using quarter, eighth and sixteenth note bass drum patterns.

In Example 31, the sixteenth bass drum beat falls between the eighth note closed hi-hat beats.

TRACKS 61+62 EXAMPLE 31

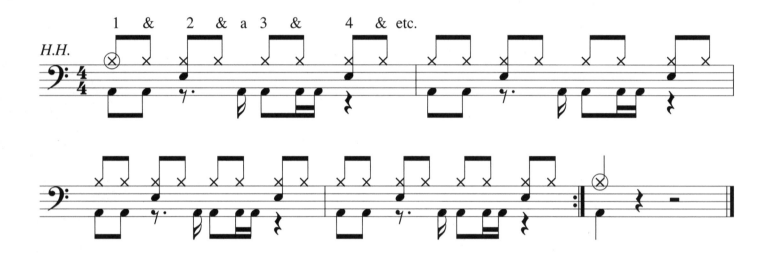

When practising these rhythms start at a slow tempo and make sure your closed hi-hat pattern remains constant and does not follow the bass drum pattern.

TRACKS 63+64 EXAMPLE 32

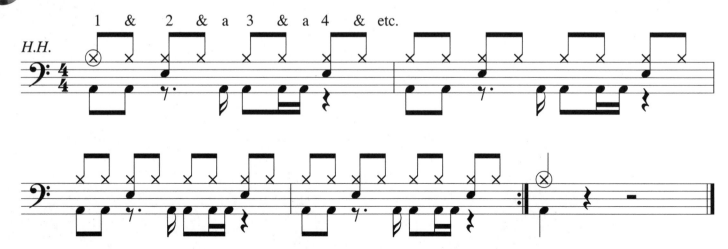

If you have any problems playing these bass
drum patterns, take a look at page 14 regarding
foot positions and the height of your drum stool.

TRACKS 65+66 **EXAMPLE 33**

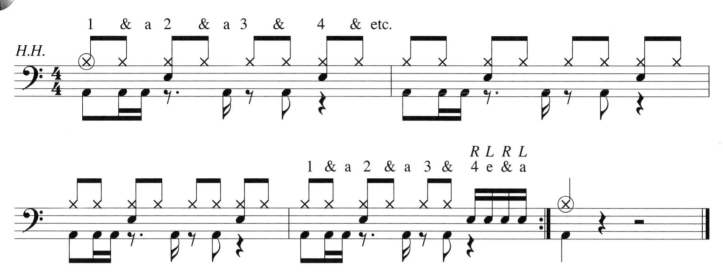

Here are three more rhythms using sixteenth
note bass drum patterns. Spend as much
time as it takes to master these rhythms,
because a good bass drum technique is essential.

TRACKS 67+68 **EXAMPLE 34**

Always try to stay as relaxed as possible.
If you become tense you will tire more easily and
limit your capabilities, as well as sounding
wooden and lumpy.

Try to set aside time to do some practise
every day rather than spending a lot of time
one day then none the next.

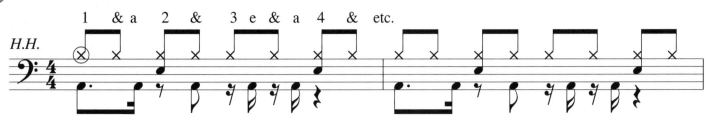

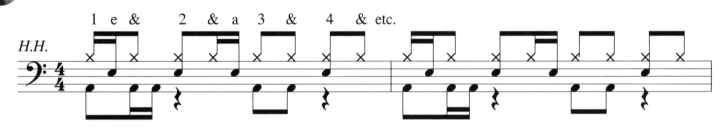

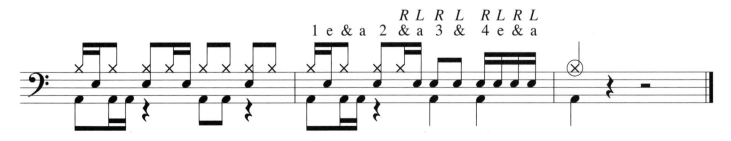

Two-Bar Rock Rhythms

All the previous rhythms have been played over one bar. In this section we will look at rhythms played over two bars.

In Example 37, we have an interesting two-bar phrase. In the first bar the bass drum plays an eighth note pattern with the snare and crash cymbal accenting the off beats.

In the second bar the bass drum does not play on the first beat but falls on the '&' of beat 1.

TRACKS 73+74 **EXAMPLE 37**

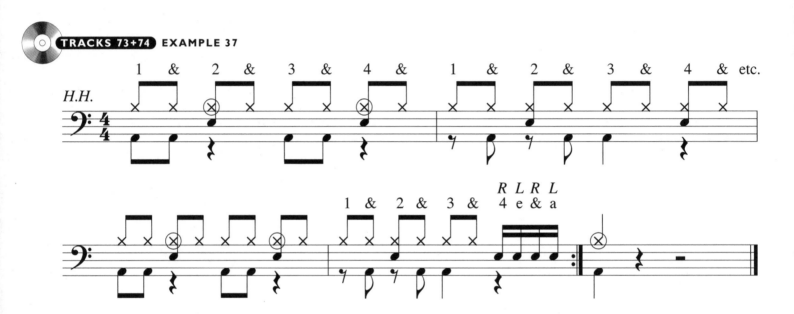

In Example 38, the first and second bars are almost the same except for the syncopated snare beat on the 'a' after beat 3 in the second bar.

TRACKS 75+76 **EXAMPLE 38**

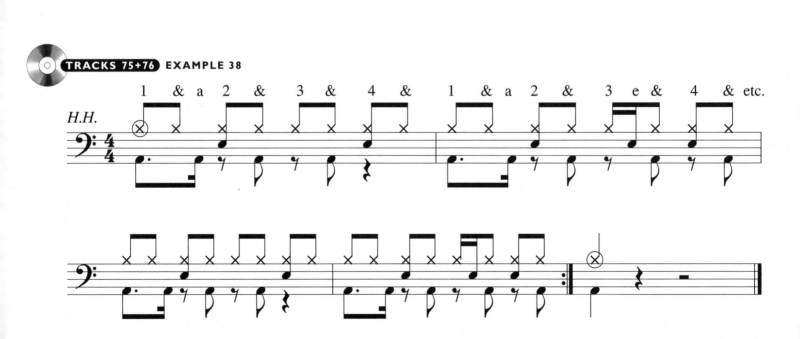

Here are three more two-bar rhythms.

Having practised them as written try experimenting with them as discussed in Chapter 1.

For example, play the closed hi-hat pattern on the ride cymbal or floor-tom and the snare notes as side stick beats.

TRACKS 77+78 **EXAMPLE 39**

In Example 40, we have a two-bar rhythm using a quarter note cymbal pattern.

TRACKS 79+80 **EXAMPLE 40**

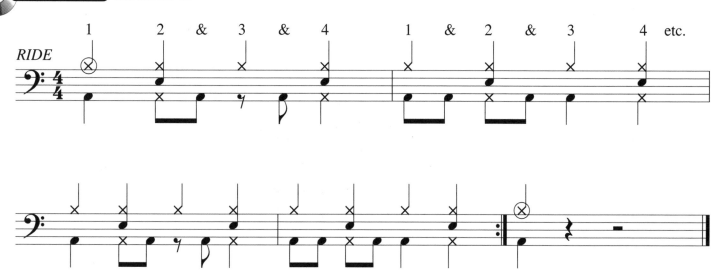

In the first bar of this two-bar rhythm, the
'a' before beat 3 is played on the snare drum.

In the second bar the 'a' is played on the
bass drum. This kind of subtle change makes the
rhythm interesting while keeping the basic
feel the same.

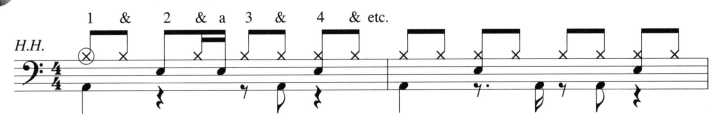

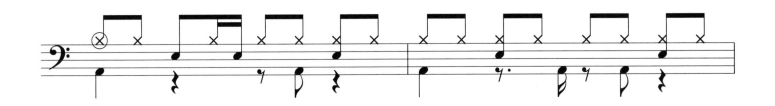

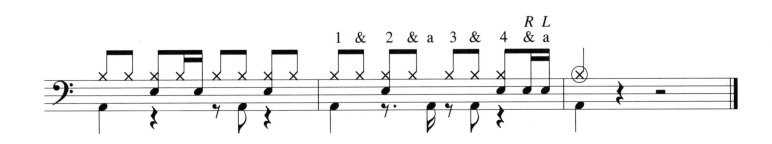

Crash Cymbal Accents On Different Beats

So far most of the crash cymbal beats
we have played have fallen on the first beat of
the bar. In this section we will look at placing the
crash cymbal on different beats of the bar.

In example 42, we have a rhythm played
over two bars with a crash on the & of beat 4
and on beat 1.

Note: Generally whenever a cymbal crash is
played, a bass drum note is played at the same
time to add some depth of sound.

TRACKS 83+84 EXAMPLE 42

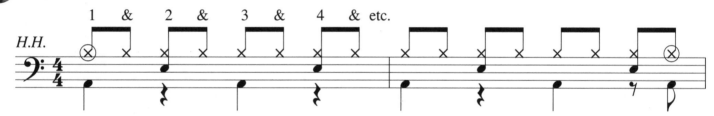

In Example 43, we have a rhythm played
over two bars with a cymbal crash on the '&' of
beat 4 in the second bar which is tied* over to
the first beat of the following bar.

This type of accented note is often called a
'push' and is very effective when the whole band
play the push together.

TRACKS 85+86 **EXAMPLE 43**

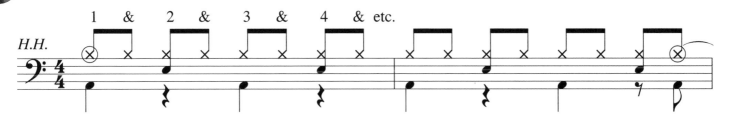

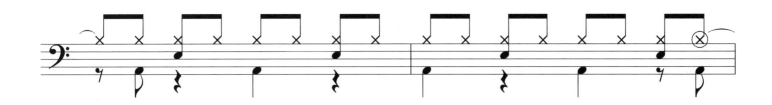

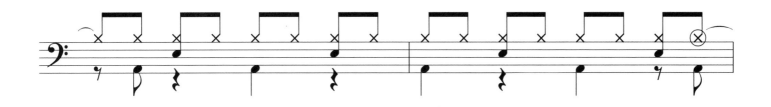

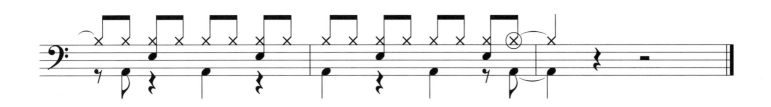

** When you see a tie joining two notes it means the
first note is played and allowed to last until the second
note is reached, so you strike only the first note.*

In Example 44, we have a cymbal crash on the last sixteenth note of bar four leading into the crash on the first beat of the following bar.

If you have two crash cymbals it is very effective playing the two from left to right in succession.

Note: The first crash is played with your left hand and the second crash is played with your right hand.

TRACKS 87+88 **EXAMPLE 44**

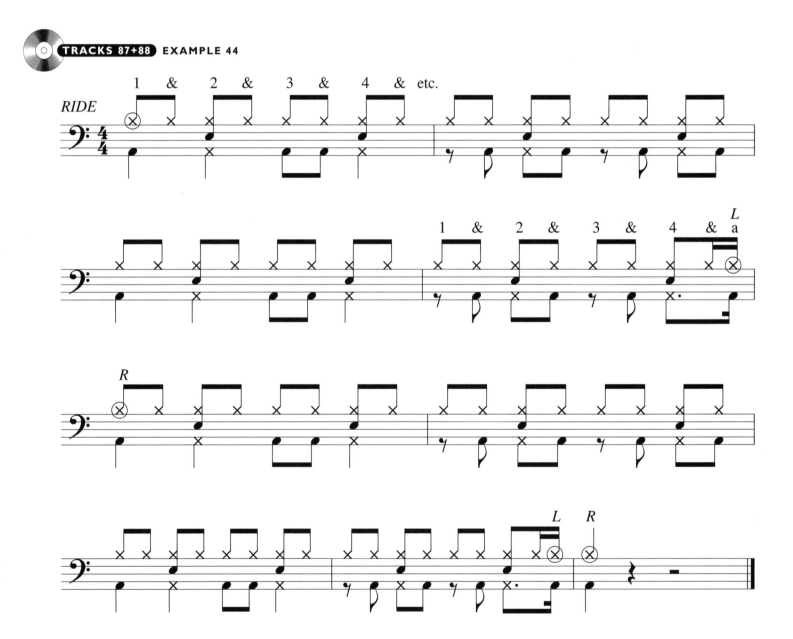

In Example 45, we have a rhythm played over two bars with a sixteenth note crash cymbal falling on the 'a' after beat 4 in the second bar.

This can sound very effective when the whole band play the accented note together.

TRACKS 89+90 **EXAMPLE 45**

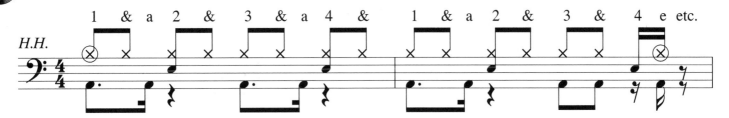

In Example 46, we have a four-bar phrase (which is repeated) using an eighth note crash cymbal push into the second bar, and a sixteenth note crash cymbal on the 'a' of beats 2 and 4 in the fourth bar.

Note: There is an eighth note rest on beat 1 in the fourth bar. To help you keep good time with this example (and all the other examples in this book) say the count that is written above the notes out loud.

TRACKS 91+92 **EXAMPLE 46**

Summary

So this brings us to the last example in this book. Example 47, is a piece of music constructed of six sections: A B C D E F

Section $\boxed{A}$ is an eight-bar intro in which we play a two-bar rhythm on the tom-toms with accents on the snare drum. Note the push in bar 8 leading into section B

In section $\boxed{B}$ we play the main riff for sixteen bars. This is a rhythm played over four bars with an interesting bass drum pattern. Note how the bass drum pattern locks in with the bass guitar.

Section $\boxed{C}$ is a four-bar bridge leading into the guitar solo. This has a half-time feel with the snare falling on beat 3.

Section $\boxed{D}$ is a sixteen-bar guitar solo. Here we play a quarter note ride cymbal pattern with a drum fill in bar 36.

In section $\boxed{E}$ we repeat the four-bar bridge as in section C

In section $\boxed{F}$ we return to the main riff as played in section B but with added syncopated snare beats in bars 50, 54, 58, 62.

Make sure you keep counting through the ending at bars 64–68.

THE HANDEL AND HAYDN SOCIETY

Bringing Music to Life for 200 Years

HANDEL AND HAYDN SOCIETY

in association with DAVID R. GODINE · PUBLISHER

First published in 2014 by

DAVID R. GODINE · *Publisher*

Post Office Box 450, Jaffrey, New Hampshire 03452 · *www.godine.com*

HANDEL AND HAYDN SOCIETY

9 Harcourt Street, Boston, Massachusetts 02116 · *www.handelandhaydn.org*

PHOTOGRAPHY CREDITS

Every effort has been made to acknowledge the photographers and copyright holders.

All images are by Julian Bullitt, Kyle Thomas Hemingway Dickinson, James Doyle, Emily Yoder Reed, and Stephen Stinehour, with the exception of the following:

Liz Linder: Cover, pp. [ii], 4, 114; Stu Rosner: pp. 2, 37, 78, 139, 200 bottom, 202, 203 bottom, 204 right, 205, 217, 218; Michael Lutch: pp. 3, 100, 200 middle, 207, 208, 215; Map reproduction courtesy of the Norman B. Leventhal Map Center at the Boston Public Library: p. 11; Courtesy of the Trustees of the Boston Public Library/Rare Books: 12, 26, 52, 53, 62; Johann Christian Rauschner, American, 1760–after 1812, Portrait of Johann Christian Gottlieb Graupner, Object Place: Boston, Massachusetts, United States, about 1810, Colored wax, 10.16 × 7.62 cm (4 × 3 in.), Museum of Fine Arts, Boston, Gift of Miss Louise C. D. Stoddard, 12.1094: p. 13 left; Johann Christian Rauschner, American, 1760–after 1812, Portrait of Mrs. Catherine C. Hillier Graupner, Object Place: Boston, Massachusetts, United States, about 1810, Colored wax, 11.11 × 7.62 cm (4⅜ × 3 in.), Museum of Fine Arts, Boston, Gift of Miss Louise C. D. Stoddard, 12.1095: p. 13 right; Courtesy of the Trustees of the Boston Public Library: pp. 28, 68, 89; Jeremy Hartman: p. 36 lower left; Gretjen Helene: pp. 36 right, 110, 113 bottom, 222 left and right, 224 bottom; 1890 engraving by H.L. Everett, courtesy of King's Chapel, Boston: p. 46; Evan Raczynski: p. 47; Courtesy of the Boston Athenæum: p. 81; Courtesy of the American Antiquarian Society: p. 90; Diane

B. Gifford Photos: p. 104; Caroline A. Cranch, John Knowles Paine (1839-1906), c. 1885-1890, Oil on canvas; 46.3 × 39.1 cm (18¼ × 15⅜ in.), framed: 26.8 × 23.8 × 11.4 cm (10⁹⁄₁₆ × 9⅜ × 4½ in.), Harvard Art Museums/Fogg Museum, Harvard University Portrait Collection, Bequest of Mrs. Mary E. Paine to Harvard College, 1920, H243, Photo: Imaging Department © President and Fellows of Harvard College: p. 128; Courtesy of Dr. Luigi Bellofato: p. 134 right; Eric Antoniou: pp. 141 top, 212 bottom, 213, 224 middle; Courtesy of the New England Conservatory Archives, p. 148; Lincoln Russell: p. 152 top right; Susan Lapides: p. 152 lower right; Courtesy of the Boston Symphony Orchestra: p. 152 lower left; Martha Hatch Bancroft: pp. 156, 185; Fabian Bachrach: p. 161; Airport Photo Service: p. 171; Fredrik D. Bodin: pp. 174, 183, 197; Newsome & Company, Inc.: p. 178; Bohdan Hrynewych: p. 187; Michael Romanos: p. 200 top; Jay R. Phillips: p. 204 left; Tom Brazil: p. 209; Stephanie Berger: p. 212 top; Maria Plati: p. 222 center; Roger Farrington: p. 224 top

Special thanks to: American Antiquarian Society; Boston Athenæum; *Boston Globe*; *Boston Herald*; Boston Public Library, Rare Books and Manuscripts Division; Boston Symphony Orchestra; Ferreira Indexing; Harvard University; King's Chapel, Boston; Museum of Fine Arts, Boston; Library of Congress; New England Conservatory; New York Public Library; Herb Boothroyd; Bridget Carr; Michelle Chiles; Brian Hayslett; Ira Pedlikin; Trevor W. Pollack; Kimberly Reynolds

LIBRARY OF CONGRESS CATALOGING-IN-PUBLICATION DATA

The Handel and Haydn Society : bringing music to life for 200 years / edited by Teresa M. Neff and Jan Swafford.
  pages cm
Includes index.
TRADE EDITION ISBN 978-1-56792-524-1 (alk. paper)
SPECIAL EDITION ISBN 978-1-56792-533-3 (alk. paper)

1. Handel and Haydn Society (Boston, Mass.)
I. Neff, Teresa M., editor. II. Swafford, Jan, editor.
ML200.8.B72H334 2014
780.6'074461—dc23
2014020032

FIRST EDITION · *Printed in China*

Dedicated to the passionate listeners and performers

who have helped to shape the Handel and Haydn Society

over the past 200 years—and to those who will define its future

CONTENTS

PREFACE

In Boston, in the early nineteenth century, a group of entrepreneurial music lovers formed the Handel and Haydn Society in the spirit of recognizing the importance of excellent music to the well-being and civic life of the young American democracy. Two hundred years later, H&H enjoys a rich history central to the development and enjoyment of classical music in this country. It is a great privilege to lead this revered institution, considered America's oldest performing arts organization in continuous existence and a national leader in both early music performance and education.

The Handel and Haydn Society today continues the vision of its founders. As H&H enters its third century, we aim to enrich life and influence culture by performing Baroque and Classical music at the highest levels of artistic excellence and by providing enlightening music education activities.

H&H is widely known for its concert series at Boston's Symphony Hall and Jordan Hall, as well as tours, local and national radio broadcasts, and recordings. Since 1854, H&H has presented Handel's *Messiah* annually, becoming part of many individual and family traditions. Times have changed and so has H&H, but, as we enter a new century, our two-fold commitment to engage all audiences through performance and to foster the creativity of young performers with unparalleled education and vocal training programs remains our fundamental goal.

Two hundred years of history provides a wealth of stories to share in a single book, and we hope that you treasure this project and its discoveries. It is with the deepest gratitude that we acknowledge the tremendous work of our tireless editors, Teresa Neff and Jan Swafford, and the team of gifted and inspired authors who have assembled this fascinating collection on the history and people of the Society. We also thank our Board members and supporters who made the book possible, particularly Amy Anthony, chair of the Bicentennial Committee, and recognize the outstanding leadership of Emily Yoder Reed, Director of Bicentennial and Community Engagement.

Our final thanks go to the patrons of the Handel and Haydn Society, who for two centuries have given purpose and meaning to our work. Your passion and enthusiasm have always been at the heart of H&H and will continue to define the future.

MARIE-HÉLÈNE BERNARD HARRY CHRISTOPHERS
Executive Director/CEO *Artistic Director*

INTRODUCTION

BOSTON'S HANDEL AND HAYDN SOCIETY enfolds the stories of many thousands of people, performers, and listeners alike, who devoted themselves to one purpose: experiencing beautiful music. We wanted our account of H&H's history—a kaleidoscopic spectacle encompassing two centuries—to be rich in anecdotes and individuals and illustrations. It is not possible to recount all of these stories in one book, so we offer a selection representing the diverse history of the Society, which became a vital part of the ascent of classical music not only in New England, but in the entire country.

In this book a series of perspectives on the Society and its history are shared by well-known scholars and musicians. As in any history, some stories rise to prominence, others are only suggested. To a large extent, each chapter stands on its own; you may read the book cover to cover, or in bits as they strike you. In the course of these chapters you will find some individuals and accounts returning, as the authors examine from different angles their parts in the Society's larger story.

As you read this history, either as a whole or as stand-alone chapters, you see that in the nineteenth century H&H was built on dynasties, from familial to conducting. Many of these figures were colorful; some were historic beyond the scope of H&H. The H&H of the twentieth century, on the other hand, was a time of eras, each conductor and Board president placing his or her own personal stamp on the organization.

Throughout its history, the idea of old and new never left the Society's mission. Beginning in 1815, in choosing its namesake composers Handel, representing older music, and Haydn, newer, to its twentieth-century practice of programming and commissioning new music to be performed alongside that of the eighteenth century, H&H has never forgotten its heritage, while maintaining a balance—an evolving balance—in its focus.

OPPOSITE
Sold-out H&H
performance at
Symphony Hall,
2011

1

In the first chapter, Jan Swafford provides an overview of the whole history of the Society, placing the organization in the context of its Boston and New England roots in singing schools and societies. Michael Broyles follows H&H through the nineteenth century, including the musical practices at the time of its founding. The many Handel premieres and the role of H&H in the development of classical music in America are shown in light of its involvement in the political and historical events of the city and country.

One of the Society's first goals, in 1815, was to promote good singing. The next two chapters break the chronological organization of the book by focusing on specific aspects of H&H's history. Matthew Guerrieri traces H&H's role as leader in music education, from 1815 to 2014, including its impact as a publisher of music collections in the early nineteenth century. Those who lead the Society, both on the stage and off, are its lifeblood; Teresa M. Neff relates H&H's history through individual profiles. Against a chronological backdrop, she describes many of the remarkable Bostonians who have contributed to the Society since 1815.

Steven Ledbetter continues the story with Handel and Haydn in the twentieth century. He begins just before the Society's move to Symphony Hall, in October 1900, then follows its Centennial in 1915, collaborations with the Boston Symphony, and first recordings and television broadcasts.

Donald Teeters, once an assistant conductor to Thomas Dunn, recounts Dunn's tenure as H&H music director and his introduction of early music practices, notably reducing the size of the chorus. But not all of Dunn's work was about the past—he also explored new works and collaborations.

With the arrival of Christopher Hogwood, the Society's Historically Informed Performance (HIP) era took firm hold. Thomas Forrest Kelly chronicles this transformation, highlighting the four conducting eras since 1986: Christopher Hogwood (1986–2001); Grant Llewellyn (2001–2006); Sir Roger Norrington (2006–2008); and Harry Christophers (2009–present).

H&H Period Instrument Orchestra and Chorus performing at Symphony Hall, 2001

This book was conceived and patiently shepherded by Handel and Haydn's Executive Director, Marie-Hélène Bernard. In bringing it to press, what resonated most with all of us was how closely the story of H&H—this story of music—touched not only important events in Boston and American history, but also people. Society members, no matter the time period, were active in many aspects of civic and cultural life; H&H's story brings new light to, and an awareness of, these times. The membership, even during the inevitable times of controversy and difficulty, believed in bringing the best music and performances to others, whether to entertain, enlighten, educate, inspire, or all these together. Its historic success in realizing this goal is the Handel and Haydn Society's legacy to uphold through the future.

TERESA M. NEFF   JAN SWAFFORD
Editor   *Editor*

OPPOSITE
H&H Period Instrument Orchestra and Chorus performing at Symphony Hall, 2013

PAGES 6–7
Performing on the Esplanade in Boston, 1987

Messiah banner outside H&H offices in Boston

JAN SWAFFORD

TWO HUNDRED YEARS: AN OVERVIEW

> I must study Politicks and War that my sons may have liberty to study Mathematicks and Philosophy. My sons ought to study Mathematicks and Philosophy…in order to give their children a right to study Painting, Poetry, Musick, and Architecture.
>
> JOHN ADAMS

THE STORY of the Boston Handel and Haydn Society in the course of its two hundred years is part of the story of music in its city and music in the United States, which on the whole traced the path founding father John Adams imagined in the late eighteenth century. At its inception, H&H was not a unique organization, but rather part of a burgeoning New England tradition. In the next centuries, what became unique about the Society was its ability to remake itself again and again from the often musically unlettered amateurs of its founding to its current position as a professional organization and world leader in historically informed performance.

In other words, the history of H&H tracks the history of classical music on this continent. Here it has been a leader, there a follower. As this book will trace, the musical thread holding together these two centuries of music has been one work that has occupied H&H from the beginning to the present: Handel's magnificent *Messiah*.

In 1800, Boston was a town of some twenty-five thousand people. To the west, in rural Massachusetts, the territory was isolated homesteads, the daily symphony hooting owls and barking foxes. Nowhere in the United States was there an orchestra, an opera house, an established conservatory of music. Naturally, there was music everywhere: wherever you find people, you find music. But in the newly minted country, the music heard was mainly a matter of jigs and reels at dances and hymns in church. Unremarked on the periphery was the African-based music of slaves and the ancient musical traditions of Native Americans.

By 1900, those same areas of western Massachusetts would be dotted in farms, not far away would reside a symphony orchestra, and the United States would be humming with music of all varieties. The story of the arts in the American nineteenth

century is a matter of outsized personalities, enthusiasm outrunning experience, and rampant can-doism. Beginning with mostly amateur fiddlers and fifers and bawling congregations, by the end of the century, Boston, like other major American cities, had a world-class orchestra, an opera house, and an important conservatory. At the same time, African-American spirituals and ragtime were conquering the globe.

When the Pilgrims landed at Plymouth Rock in 1620, they had with them a psalter with a few tunes. In 1640, the first book published in English in North America was the *Bay Psalm Book*, consisting of thirteen hymns printed with woodblocks. The first eight editions of the book had only words, because hardly anyone could read music. Progress from that point was sluggish. In 1800, in Europe, Beethoven published his first string quartets, and Joseph Haydn, having just finished his massive oratorio *The Creation*, premiered his equally massive *The Seasons*. In America, meanwhile, the major musical publications of that year were six hymnals, a collection of odes on the death of George Washington, and one instruction book each for singers and instrumentalists.

Well into the eighteenth century, the state of hymn singing in churches, to those sensitive to music, was best described as excruciating. As one pained hearer put it, singing in church was "a scandalous mockery of psalmody, led by a barrel organ or an incompetent professor." Starting in the 1720s, in New England, there was a movement to improve singing and musical literacy in churches. In 1721, Reverend

Map of
BOSTON
in the State of
MASSACHUSETTS
Surveyd by J. G. Hales
Geog.r & Surveyor
1814

WARD N.º 7

WARD N.º 6

MILL POND

WARD N.º 3

WARD N.º 4

WATER ST

WARD N.º 5

WARD N.º 2

WARD N.º 9

Franklin Place

WARD N.º 8

COMMON

WARD N.º 11

WARD N.º 12

C H A R L E S   R I V E R

BEACON STREET

The Theatre

LONG WHARF

EAST STREET India Wharf

B O S T O N   H A R B O U R

South Boston Bridge

WASHINGTON STREET

Dorchester Street

Explanation

An artistic presentation of a four-part hymn on the first page of *The Continental Harmony*, published by William Billings in 1794, with the explanation, "This tune is thus disposal to shew that every tune is a Compleat circle; & that what may be deficient in the first barr is supplied in the last."

T. Walter published *An Introduction to the Art of Singing by Note*, whose introduction complained that congregational singing "had become so mutilated, tortured, and twisted, that psalm singing had become a mere disorderly noise, left to the mercy of every unskillful throat."

Thus began the singing-school movement that grew through the eighteenth century and into the nineteenth, which developed into more ambitious singing societies that became the foundation of musical endeavors including the Handel and Haydn Society. In 1807, fifteen Boston gentlemen founded the Massachusetts Musical Society, each member donating two dollars to purchase a musical library including Handel's *Messiah* and music by Mozart. By then, singing schools and societies had become a conduit for the introduction of European classical music into the United States. In effect, the musical development of American culture and the extraordinary profusion of music that exists here now began in large part with the struggles of early Americans to get people to read music and sing better in church.

Associated with the singing-school movement was America's first significant composer, Boston's William Billings (1746–1800). Self-taught in music, Billings largely wrote hymns in four parts that were rough and ready in harmony and archaic in layout: the tune was in the tenor line and the parts were sung by both men and women, so everything came out in octaves. Billings became a vital part of the church-music reform movement of the late eighteenth century; his tunes are still sung and enjoyed. But as often happens to artists and politicians, the reform inaugurated by the next generation of New England musicians turned against Billings, toward a more "proper" and "scientific" style that followed old-world rules. That reform would also play its part in the early years of H&H.

Given the nature of America as an immigrant country, in the eighteenth century there had been a steady trickle of music and musical forums making their way to the new world. The first documented public concert in the United States was heard in Boston in 1731. Thrilled by the concert life during his sojourn in Europe, Thomas Jefferson played violin and called music "the favorite passion of my soul." A seminal figure in Boston concert life was German-born Gottlieb Graupner, who arrived in 1797. He had once played oboe under Haydn in London. In 1809, he formed the Philo-Harmonic Society; this small group of mostly amateurs lasted until 1824, playing some Haydn alongside lighter composers. Graupner led the group from his position as its double bass player. A busy entrepreneur married to a singer, Graupner was Boston's main music publisher for some twenty-five years. Among his efforts was helping to found H&H.

Gottlieb Graupner, H&H founder and leader of the orchestra, and Catherine Hillier Graupner, one of the first soloists with the Society. Photograph © 2014 Museum of Fine Arts, Boston

How that founding came about, two centuries after the Pilgrims landed in Plymouth, began with a couple of concerts in February 1815. The first, at Rev. Dr. Baldwin's meeting house, was scheduled for the sixteenth of that month, by the Second Baptist Singing Society. The program was a selection of movements from "the most favorite authors of Europe": the first part of Haydn's *Creation* and works by Handel, including the "Hallelujah" Chorus from *Messiah* and part of *Judas Maccabaeus.* Since word had just been received of the peace agreement ending the War of 1812, the concert became something of a celebration of the event. In its comment, *The Advertiser* particularly rhapsodized over "the rare and astonishingly sublime and descriptive production of Haydn, which has never been exhibited in New England." *The Creation* was immensely popular in Europe in those days, and it would prove likewise in the United States. The first part of the oratorio ends with its grandest and most famous chorus, "The Heavens are Telling the Glory of God."

That occasion having gone well, a second was mounted on February 22, this one intended to celebrate both George Washington's birthday and the end of the war. A procession marched from the State House to historic King's Chapel, where a large and enthusiastic audience again heard choruses of Handel and Haydn presented by a collection of two hundred and fifty singers and instrumentalists. It was agreed that such concerts were a fine idea, so why not continue them?

After the second concert, Gottlieb Graupner, Thomas Smith Webb, and Aaron (Asa) Peabody issued a call for interested parties to meet in regard to "cultivating and improving a correct taste in the performance of sacred music." In March 1815, two meetings were held, the first not on record, the second at Graupner's Hall, attended by sixteen men. They agreed to form an oratorio society, with Handel and Haydn at the heart of the repertoire. In April, the members drafted a fervent constitution. It began:

> While in our country almost every institution, political, civil and moral, has advanced with rapid steps, while every other science is cultivated with a success flattering to its advocates, the admirers of music find their beloved science far from exciting the feelings or exercising the powers to which it is accustomed in the Old World. Too long have those to whom heaven has given a voice to perform and an ear that can enjoy music neglected a science which has done much towards subduing the ferocious passions of men and giving innocent pleasure to society; and so absolute has been their neglect, that most of the works of the greatest composers of sacred music have never found those in our land who have even attempted their performance. Impressed with these sentiments, the undersigned do hereby agree to form themselves into a society, by the name of the Handel and Haydn Society, for the purpose of improving the style of performing sacred

Park Street Church, Boston

music, and introducing into more general use the works of Handel and Haydn and other eminent composers.

At that point there were forty-four members who signed the constitution and contributed $53 (some $750 in modern dollars) toward music and other expenses. Most of these founders were veterans of local church choirs, especially the well-trained group at Park Street Church. It was agreed that members must have good singing voices, though it was considered too much to require them to know how to read music. None of the men was a Boston Brahmin, but rather entirely middle-class. Many were merchants; the rest represented a mélange of professions from bank cashier to shopkeeper to printer to apothecary. Only two are listed as professional musicians, one being Gottlieb Graupner. From that beginning, H&H remained predominately a middle-class organization whose goals were as much pleasure and self-improvement as performance. From among the founders, Thomas Smith Webb was named president of the Society, which made him at the same time music director in theory, if not always in practice.

Christmas Day, 1815 marked the first Handel and Haydn Society performance at King's Chapel. It was an auspicious start for what no one could have imagined was going to become a history encompassing centuries. The audience numbered around a thousand, the chorus ninety men and ten women, supported by a small instrumental group and organ. The program was a huge compendium in three

SELECT ORATORIO,

AS PERFORMED BY THE

HANDEL AND HAYDN SOCIETY,

AT KING'S CHAPEL, IN BOSTON,

ON THE EVENING OF *CHRISTMAS,*

DECEMBER 25, 1815.

BOSTON;

C. Stebbins, Printer.

1815.

67th Season.   635th Concert.

Handel and Haydn Society.

BOSTON MUSIC HALL,

GOOD FRIDAY,

APRIL 7, 1882,

AT 3 O'CLOCK, P. M.

PASSION MUSIC,

ACCORDING TO SAINT MATTHEW.

FIRST PART.

MRS. E. ALINE OSGOOD, SOPRANO.

MISS MATHILDE PHILLIPPS, CONTRALTO.

MR. WILLIAM J. WINCH, TENOR.

MR. JOHN F. WINCH, BASS.

MR. GEORG HENSCHEL, BASS.

MR. CARL ZERRAHN, CONDUCTOR.

MR. B. LISTEMANN, SOLO AND LEADING VIOLINIST.

MR. B. J. LANG, ORGANIST.

MR. H. G. TUCKER, PIANIST.

CHOIR OF BOYS FROM THE PUBLIC SCHOOLS,

TRAINED BY MR. JOSEPH B. SHARLAND.

THIS EVENING, at 8 o'clock, Second Part of the *Saint Matthew Passion*.

APRIL 9 (EASTER SUNDAY). HAYDN'S *The Creation*. Solos by Miss FANNY KELLOGG, Mr. TOM KARL, Mr.
MYRON W. WHITNEY. Reserved Seats at $1.00 and $1.50 each, according to location, now ready.

like, though they could rehearse for H&H. Henschel was an outstanding baritone; he and his American wife, soprano Lillian June Bailey, often soloed with the Society.

In 1900, Boston's Symphony Hall was inaugurated and soon proved itself one of the world's great concert halls. It became the home of both the Boston Symphony and H&H. While from the beginning Higginson's orchestra provided cheap "rush" seats and popular concerts that evolved into the Pops, the orchestra was essentially an aristocratic organization. As was said toward the end of the century: "Whatever popularizes, vulgarizes." By that point there was a rigid and highly elite divide between "high" and "low" art, and the former was pursued with a kind of religious devotion. Courtenay Guild, who became H&H president in 1915, deplored syncopated dance music as "a sort of barbarous sequence of sounds that is more worthy of savages than of civilization."

But H&H was on the move. The twentieth century saw an expansion into continually new repertoire (with *Messiah* still a constant), into performances of contemporary works, including H&H commissions, and a steady ascent in the level of music-making. The advent of Music Director Thomas Dunn, in 1967, brought a historic new era: balanced programming of early and contemporary works, including premieres; a new concern with historically informed performance (still on modern instruments); and a turn away from the giant choruses of the past to a smaller and more highly trained choir. His December 1972 *Messiah* performance had a choir of thirty. After Dunn's long tenure, with the advent of Christopher Hogwood as music director in 1986, the turn toward an historically informed ensemble with period instruments was complete. The Society's first period-ensemble recording of *Messiah* was released in 2000. By then the chorus consisted entirely of paid professionals.

Today the Handel and Haydn Society occupies a leading place among performing organizations in the United States, recording and performing around the world. The 2000s saw the ascent of Grant Llewellyn and Harry Christophers to the podium. There was a steady broadening of repertoire and approach: the orchestra's San Francisco collaboration with the vocal ensemble Chanticleer for the world premiere and recording of John Tavener's *Lamentations and Praises*; fully staged productions of

OPPOSITE TOP: H&H time capsule, 1865. "This box contains a full file of the Boston Post Daily Advertiser and Boston Transcript during the Festival week, May 23 to 28th 1865 with full notices of the same. Also Watson's Art Journal of New York with a full report of the entire Festival; and a pamphlet containing the programs of all the oratorios and concerts, together with the names of the officers of the Society, the assisting artists both vocal & instrumental and of the chorus. Also a copy of Dwight's Journal of Music with reports of officers at Annual Meeting. Not to be opened till the 100th Anniversary of the Society in 1915. —Loring B Barnes, Sect." Unfortunately, the box was forgotten in 1915 and the "Lost Box," as it was later termed, was not opened until 1940.

OPPOSITE BELOW: *The Boston Daily Globe*, April 8, 1940

This I Box contains

A full file of the Boston Post, Daily Advertiser and Boston Transcript, during the Festival week of May 23 to 28th 1865, with full notices of the same. Also Watson's Art Journal of New York with a full report of the entire Festival; and a pamphlet containing the programmes of all the oratorios & concerts, together with the names of the officers of the Society, the assisting Artists both Vocal & Instrumental, and of the Chorus. Also a copy of Dwight's Journal of Music with reports of officers at Annual Meeting.

Not to be opened 'till the 100th Anniversary of the Society in 1915.

[signed] B. Barnes, Sect.

Handel and Haydn Society Open Box Sealed in 1865

OPENING THE "LOST" BOX
Left to Right—James T. Gearon, Dr. Thompson Stone, Courtenay Guild and Paul F. Spain.

By JANET JONES

The "lost" box of the Handel and Haydn Society—sealed at its 50th anniversary in 1865 to be opened at its 100th in 1915, but believed lost until it was found last December in a safe at Symphony Hall—was opened last night at the society's rehearsal for its 125th concert on April 15.

In the box were several copies of Boston newspapers of that period, each containing reviews of the Handel and Hadyn Festival of May 25-28, 1865, a copy of Watson's Art Journal of New York, a pamphlet containing the programs of all the oratorios and concerts given, together with the names of the officers of the society, the assisting artists and the chorus, a copy of Dwight's Journal of Music and reports of the officers at the July annual meeting.

One paper criticized the Festival, which was held at the old Music Hall, for its choice of songs. Since this was just about a month after the assassination of Lincoln and the end of the Civil War, the reviewer blasted:

". . . The ill-founded education of the time was clearly shown in the choice of songs—three out of four pieces being operatic scenes, which are well enough under ordinary circumstance, but ought at such a time as this to be set aside for lyrics which are classical and rare."

Mrs. Carey's "Twitter"

In a later reference to one of the assisting artists, the paper continued, "Mrs. Cary gave an aria from 'Giuramento' with quite brilliant execution (all but her trill, which has not passed beyond what may be called the twitter period.)"

The orchestra, which the reviewer called "the band" throughout, apparently saved the day when it "played from memory the accompaniment to 'Robert,' when Mr. Cutler gave it up because he had carelessly brought an imperfect copy to the piano. But for their timely and capable intervention, the aria would have been hopelessly broken down."

The announcement that Boston was to hold such a Festival, said the tony Watson's Art Journal of New York, "created much conversation and not a little jocular comment in this city. The mildly conceited and knowing ones poopooh'd the affair gracefully as a provincial concern—as a one-horse arrangement of psalm singers which could be made something of if Mr. This or That of New York were to take it in hand and put it through."

Four Men Open Box

Messrs. Courtenay Guild, the society's president; Dr. Thompson Stone, conductor; Paul F. Spain, vice president, and James T. Gearon, secretary, opened the box on the stage of the Y. W. C. A. auditorium, in the presence of 250 choristers. Also at the ceremony was Boston composer, Miss Mabel Daniels, daughter of the late George Frank Daniels, a former president of the society. Miss Daniels said that as both her father and mother had once sung in the chorus, she thought that was probably the place where their courtship got its start.

The papers of those four days, May 25 to 28, were filled with accounts of Booth's trial, reviews of Sheridan's army, "The sublimest military campaign of the 19th century," as one captain called it, editorials on "The Perils of Peace" and multitudinous advertisements.

Two women members of the chorus picked up one of the papers—which all sold for 5 cents, and were just four pages long—and exclaimed, "What! No funnies?"

But then they saw an ad which amused them. In bold letters it called attention to "The Great Invention of the Age—Hoop Skirts."

The Handel and Haydn Society last night also announced the gift of about 10 scores and libretti, all dated between 1823 and 1859, from Webster Tomlinson of Joliet, Ill., whose mother had sung with the society in Boston.

Vocal Arts Program performances, 2012–2013

Monteverdi's *Vespers* and *L'Orfeo* and Purcell's *Dido and Aeneas*, directed by Chen Shi-Zheng; Christophers leading the Society's continental European debut in a Haydn Festival at the Esterházy Palace in Austria, where Haydn had once worked; Sir Roger Norrington directing Haydn's *The Seasons* at Royal Albert Hall.

At the same time, the Society's Education Program, begun in 1985, has broadened steadily to include a youth choruses program and further community efforts, eventually reaching some ten thousand students a year. In 2004, the Youth Chorus sang at the Democratic National Convention in Boston. These efforts have returned the Society to its early tradition as an institution devoted to spreading the word about music and developing skills through music education.

In that respect, the modern Handel and Haydn Society has come full circle since its early years: a performing group with a vital educational program, an approach that is at the same time bottom-up and top-down. It performs for large, enthusiastic audiences that are variously in search of entertainment, edification, and inspiration. The founders of 1815 would be both astounded and proud of what has come from their little group of amateurs singing for the love of great music and for the fun of it.

H&H Period Instrument Orchestra and Chorus, Symphony Hall, 2013

PAGES 38–39
The design of the first program books for H&H
concerts was utilitarian. Later program books,
however, developed visually distinctive covers.

ORATORIO

FOR

THANKSGIVING-DAY EVENING,

DECEMBER 3d.

PERFORMED

AT

BOYLSTON HALL,

BY THE

HANDEL AND HAYDN SOCIETY.

———

BOSTON·

PRINTED BY T. BADGER, JR.
1818.

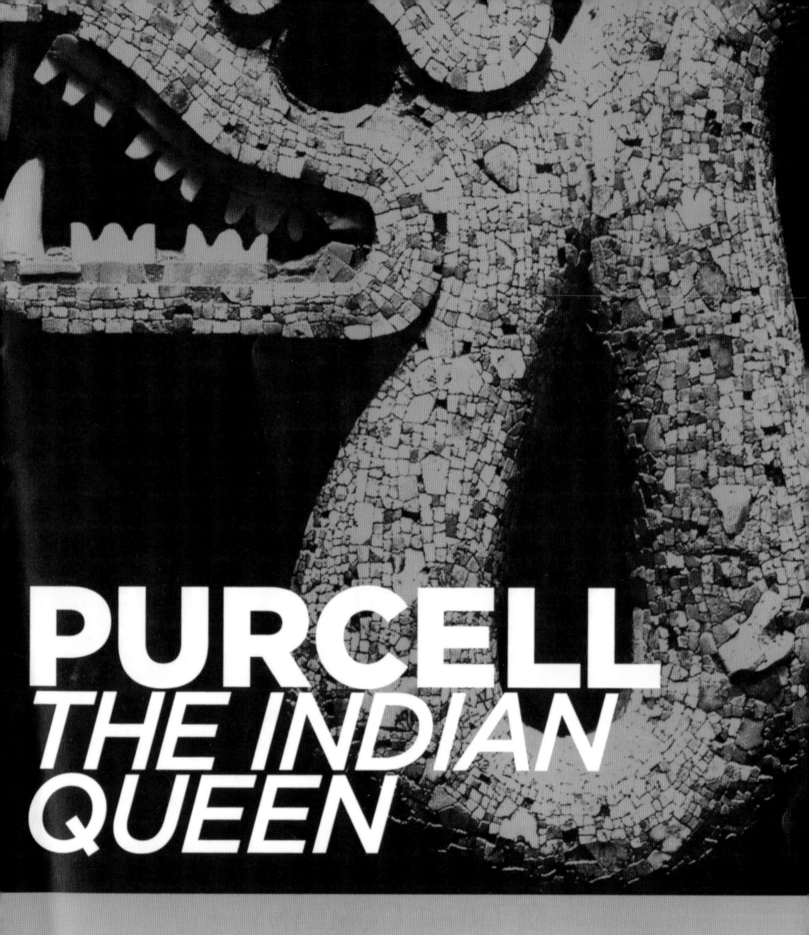

PURCELL
THE INDIAN QUEEN

JANUARY 25, 2013 AT NEC'S JORDAN HALL
JANUARY 27, 2013 AT SANDERS THEATRE

Handel | Haydn

2012–2013
198TH SEASON

HANDEL & HAYDN SOCIETY

Musical Festival!

ON THE 21st, 22d, AND 23d OF MAY. 1857

ON THURSDAY MORNING, 21st, AT 10 O'CLOCK, ADDRESS BY

HON. ROBERT C. WINTHROP,

TO BE FOLLOWED BY

HAYDN'S CREATION.

IN THE AFTERNOON AT 3 1-2 O'CLOCK,

A Miscellaneous, Orchestral and Vocal Concert.

ON FRIDAY MORNING, 22d, AT 10 1-2 O'CLOCK,

MENDELSSOHN'S ELIJAH.

And on the Afternoon, at 3 1-2 o'clock, a VOCAL and INSTRUMENTAL CONCERT, similar to the one of the day preceding.

On SATURDAY MORNING 23d, at 10 1-2 o'clock, a GRAND ORCHESTRAL and VOCAL CONCERT, and on SATURDAY EVENING, at 7 1-2 o'clock,

Handel's Messiah,

WITH A

CHORUS OF SIX HUNDRED & AN ORCHESTRA OF EIGHTY PERFORMERS.

☞ THE DOORS WILL BE OPENED ONE HOUR BEFORE THE COMMENCEMENT OF EACH PERFORMANCE. ☜

CARL ZERRAHN,..Conductor.
F. F. MÜLLER,..Organist.

Tickets, with Reserved Seats, at Five Dollars each,

For sale at Russell & Richardson's, 291 Washington Street, and SINGLE TICKETS to the separate Concerts, at One Dollar each, for sale at the same place, until WEDNESDAY EVENING, after which time the sale will be continued at the MUSIC HALL.

J. S. POTTER, PRINTER, 2 SPRING LANE.

MICHAEL BROYLES

GROWTH, CHANGE, AND DISCOVERIES IN THE NINETEENTH CENTURY

IN THE NINETEENTH CENTURY, the United States experienced monumental economic and political changes. The nation expanded from a few states along the Atlantic to a transcontinental empire, the frontier was conquered or at least formally closed, the industrial revolution reshaped many towns and cities and created vast holdings of wealth, and the thorniest issue that had faced the new nation was decided by the bloodiest war in American history.

The role of the arts, especially music, was also transformed. At the beginning of the century, professional musicians were rare and music was little more than entertainment. By the end of the century, opera and symphony were well-established, European musicians had flooded the country, American performers and composers could claim equal status with their foreign colleagues, music professorships had been created at prestigious universities, and a hierarchy of aesthetic values, which bestowed a sacrosanct status on some types of secular music, was firmly in place.

Boston's Handel and Haydn Society, which began as an institution to answer the musical needs of 1815, succeeded because it rose to new challenges brought by a rapidly shifting cultural landscape. Yet its ascent was anything but a steady climb or a smooth path. In any historical narrative there are moments of crisis, and the growth of an institution usually depends on how it handles those crises.

The story of H&H in the nineteenth century is punctuated by a series of such events. Beginning as early as 1817, there were years when the survival of the fledgling Society was imperiled, but each time it managed to rise to the occasion. Between these critical moments there were years when the Society coasted. In some cases the sheer inertia of such periods precipitated a crisis, in others the workings of the

41

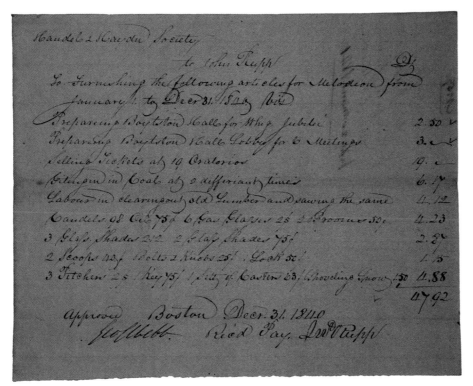

Payments made to John Rupp for "Furnishing the following articles for Melodeon from January 1. to Decr 31. 1840." The list includes "2 Scoops of Bolts & Knobs," candles, and coal, as well as selling tickets and "Labour in clearing out old Lumber and sawing the same."

Society. Several of the more important members of H&H followed him, but they did not resign. H&H, which had printed Chevalier Sigismund Neukomm's *Hymn of the Night* for its own use, was appalled when the Oratorio Society performed the same piece on the same night. The Board voted to expel Brown and the other members unless they repented, which they made clear they had no intention of doing. However, the new group, caught between internal dissension and lack of public support, soon expired.

H&H was able to improve its concert setting in 1839, when it moved to the Melodeon, a new performance hall next to where the Boston Opera House stands today. It had previously met in Boylston Hall, a general meeting room that occupied the third floor of the Boylston Market. The Melodeon was a more dedicated performance space, and the Society's contract gave it more flexibility for both rehearsals and concerts. Yet the Melodeon created further financial problems. In addition to the cost of rental, H&H spent more than $1,000 outfitting the hall for its needs.

Adding to the Society's difficulties were new musical stirrings. In 1841, symphonic music arrived in Boston. Concerts that included symphonies had occurred prior to the 1840s, but they were sporadic, and miscellaneous symphonic movements were often juxtaposed among other offerings, such as solos, duets, and trios both vocal and instrumental. A secular concert of those days was a loose amalgam of highly divergent material.

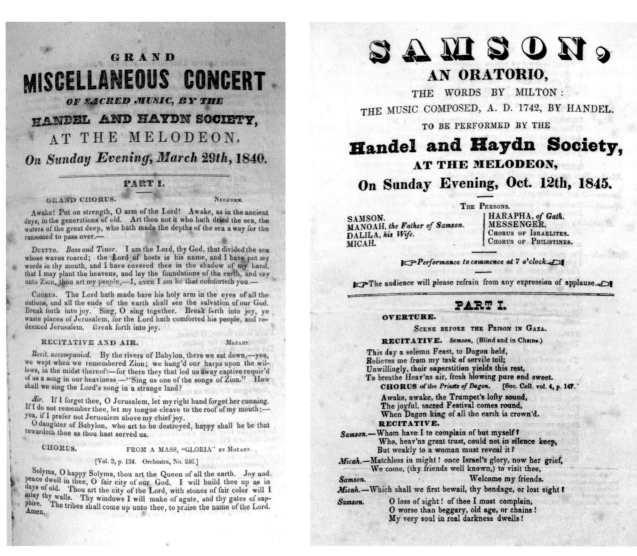

Program for March 1840 concert at the Melodeon Theater   Program for Handel's *Samson*, October 1845

By 1841, the Boston Academy of Music had formed a symphony orchestra in Boston, whose success gave rise to a second symphonic organization, the Boston Philharmonic Society (unrelated to the later Boston Symphony Orchestra), and chamber music groups. At the same time, many instrumental virtuosi arrived from Europe. With so many new and different musical offerings available, interest in oratorios dropped precipitously. One 1843 H&H performance of Mendelssohn's *St. Paul* brought in a grand total of $62.50. A subsequent series of three concerts of selections from various composers was even more disastrous, with nightly receipts of $16.00, $29.00, and $19.50. Since the Society no longer had income from publications, it found itself in severe financial straits. Drastic measures were proposed, such as dropping the orchestra and severely curtailing programs, limiting itself to only "miscellaneous programmes," rather than large works like the *Messiah* and *The Creation*.

These measures were rejected. The following year, 1845, a series of performances of Handel's *Samson*, new to Boston audiences, managed at least to stave off total collapse. The Board considered appointing a professional conductor, but chose not to, "as the president considered it inexpedient." The crisis, however, was only delayed, not averted. The Society continued to struggle into the early 1850s. Interest waned even among members. In 1852, membership was officially recorded as two hundred, but fewer than half were active. Attendance at rehearsals and concerts averaged sixty-eight. The secretary, well aware of the situation, recorded that "a faithful nucleus keeps the Society alive."

Yet because of the growth in instrumental ensembles in the 1840s, interest in concert music in Boston was at an all-time high. In November 1852, Boston Music Hall, on the corner of Winter and Tremont streets, was completed. Charles Callahan Perkins, later an H&H president, considered it "finer than any in this country, or hardly any in the Old World." Lit by gas, it held twenty-seven hundred people; a large statue of Beethoven dominated the stage. In 1863, E. F. Walcker and Company installed in the Hall the largest organ in the United States at the time.

Program for February 1853 concert
with the Germania Musical Society

If H&H was to maintain its leading position in the Boston musical scene, it needed to change, and it did—but only by accident, through a series of events that in the long run proved fortuitous. In 1852, F. F. Mueller was elected organist and George J. Webb named conductor. Organist, hymn composer, and colleague of Lowell Mason, Webb, who had served the Society since 1830, represented more the musical world of the 1830s. By the 1840s, he also directed the Musical Fund Society Orchestra.

Another ensemble, however, had appeared in town: the Germania Orchestra, which brought to America a hitherto unknown level of precision in orchestral performance. Imbued with the idealistic notion of making music in a free society, independent of the shackles of European patronage, twenty-five young German musicians formed a musical corporation in Berlin in 1848. After some time in England accruing money for the transatlantic trip, they arrived in the United States in September 1848. After touring the East Coast for several years, the Germanians took up residence in Boston, finding it most responsive to their programs.

By all accounts they were by far a better orchestra than that of the Musical Fund Society. Wanting the Germanians but not wanting to offend its conductor, Webb, the Society voted to engage the Musical Fund for three concerts and the Germania for three. The Musical Fund insisted on "all, or none" of the concerts, and the Society then voted in favor of the Germanians, whereupon the minutes record that on

November 10, 1852, Webb resigned. This allowed Carl Bergmann, cellist and conductor of the Germania Orchestra, to be appointed conductor of H&H.

Bergmann insisted on a higher level of musicianship from the chorus, and the members responded. Membership and attendance rose dramatically, possibly because of the appeal the Germanians had as a young, vibrant group of outstanding musicians. In December 1852 and January 1853, H&H gave three performances of Handel's *Judas Maccabaeus* to a packed hall, and on February 5, 1853, joined with the Germania Orchestra for the Boston premiere of Beethoven's Ninth Symphony. The chorus had by then swelled to two hundred and fifty.

In 1854, the Germanians decided to disband so that its members could pursue individual careers. Bergmann moved to Chicago and then New York, and the Society turned to another member of the orchestra, Carl Zerrahn, as its conductor. Zerrahn held the position for more than forty years, providing a musical continuity that had not been present during the Society's first decades.

A second important appointment was made in 1859, when B. J. Lang was named organist. A native of Salem, Massachusetts, Lang had gone to Europe in 1855, at age eighteen, to study composition and piano with, among others, Franz Liszt. After returning, Lang became an important member of the Boston musical world, performing as a concert pianist, organist, and conductor. In addition to his work with

Germania Musical Society: Carl Zerrahn, left, holding a flute, and Carl Bergmann, seated at center, holding a score

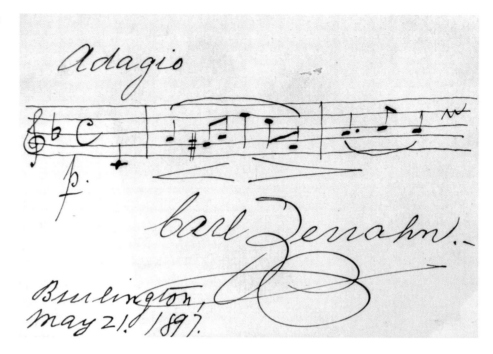

H&H, Lang conducted the Apollo Club, a men's choral group, and the Cecilia
Society, a mixed choral ensemble, and later performed frequently as pianist with the
Boston Symphony Orchestra. He continued with H&H as organist for nearly forty
years, and briefly as conductor in the 1890s.

Thus, from the 1850s into the 1890s, H&H remained relatively stable. With Bergmann, Zerrahn, and then Lang, the Society redefined itself. It was no longer the
church-related choir, reminiscent of an old singing school, that characterized its first
years; it was no longer a group of amateurs with little or no musical training who
could succeed because audiences had nothing to compare it to; it was no longer a
club that could pick its soloists from its own ranks and whose president led rehearsals and performances. In a city with a new musical environment, one that offered
multiple musical choices, both vocal and instrumental, a city whose audiences were
growing increasingly sophisticated, H&H had to change and it did. While the chorus
was still unpaid, H&H became an organization with divided duties—a president and
other administrative officers, a musical director, an organist, and a Board of Trustees,
renamed Board of Directors in 1867.

There were controversies in the second half of the century, such as a sharp division, in 1867, over whether or not to revive Rossini's opera *Moses in Egypt*, done as an
oratorio. Several newly elected members of the Board recommended it. Lang, Zerrahn, and most of the officers opposed the idea, but the Board voted narrowly, first
seven-to-five, a second time six-to-five, to perform it.

HANDEL AND HAYDN SOCIETY.

THE
FIFTH PERFORMANCE
OF THE
GRAND ORATORIO OF
MOSES IN EGYPT,

THE MUSIC BY ROSSINI,

With words translated expressly for this Society,

BY GEORGE S. PARKER, A.M.

WILL BE GIVEN

ON SUNDAY EVEN'G, FEB. 26th, 1854.

AT THE

BOSTON MUSIC HALL,

WITH THE VOCAL ASSISTANCE OF

Mr. THOMAS BALL,	- as -	PHARAOH, King of Egypt.	
Mr. A. ARTHURSON,	- - -	OSIRIS, his Son,	{ Opposed to the departure of the Israelites, from love to the daughter of Moses.
Miss ANNA STONE,	- - -	NICAULE, Queen of Egypt.	
Mr. H. M. AIKEN,	- - - -	MOSES of Israel.	
Mrs. E. A. WENTWORTH,	- -	ESTHER,	} Daughters of Moses.
Miss S. E. BROWN,	- - - -	ALMATEA,	
Mr. B. WHEAT,	- - - - -	AARON, Brother of Moses.	

WITH ORCHESTRAL ACCOMPANIMENTS BY THE

GERMANIA MUSICAL SOCIETY.

1

PART THE FIRST.

no. 1

RECITATIVE—"Now there arose."

Strings

Now there arose   a new king over Egypt, which knew not Joseph; and he set   over

Organo.
(by the Editor)

Violoncello 1mo
mf
Violoncello 2do

Pianoforte
Adaptation.

mf

mf

Israel task-masters   to afflict them with burdens; and they made them serve with rigour.

5

Only one crisis, however, threatened to rupture the Society. In 1894–1895, membership divided over Zerrahn's continuance. He was nearing seventy years of age and officers felt it was time for a change. Zerrahn voluntarily resigned and Lang was appointed conductor. In 1897, the membership, especially the younger members, revolted against the officers and voted, narrowly, to reappoint Zerrahn. The principal officers, angered at what they considered a usurpation of their authority, resigned *en masse*. After a period of considerable enmity, which spilled into the Boston newspapers, new officers were elected, supporters of Lang withdrew, and Zerrahn came back for one more year before retiring permanently. It should be noted that neither Zerrahn nor Lang was directly involved in this dispute. They had worked together for years, had a close relationship, and respected each other.

The story of H&H in the second half of the nineteenth century is primarily one of musical growth and expansion, of new venues, new occasions, new collaborations, new experiments, and new compositions. By mid-century, H&H already had established a reputation for first performances. On Christmas Day, 1818, it gave the first complete performance of *Messiah* in America, followed by the first complete performance of Haydn's *Creation* on February 16, 1819. Other American premieres before 1850 were Mozart's *Missa longa* in C in 1829, and Handel's *Samson* in 1845. Notable Boston premieres were Mendelssohn's *St. Paul* and Rossini's Stabat Mater in 1843, Handel's *Judas Maccabaeus* in 1847, and Mendelssohn's *Elijah* in 1848. Thus, by mid-century, the Society had introduced to the city much important oratorio literature, including then-recent works in the repertoire.

Premieres were not always received positively. Handel's oratorio *Israel in Egypt*, which had been lauded by Mozart and Mendelssohn, was first presented by H&H on February 13, 1859. For Boston audiences it was a flop. *The Boston Courier* wrote, "The

OPPOSITE
First page of score,
with conductor
markings, for
Handel's *Israel in
Egypt*, given to H&H
by C. F. Chickering

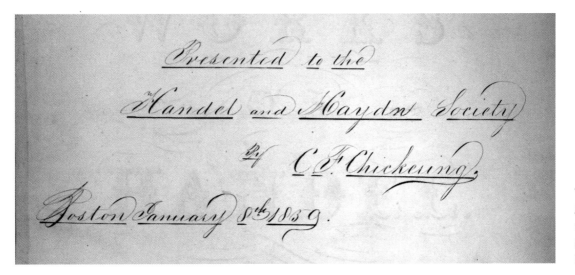

The score for Handel's
Israel in Egypt "presented
to the Handel and Haydn
Society by C. F. Chickering,
Boston January 8th 1839"

undivided performance of even the best of Handel's oratorios is an infliction too severe for modern audiences to endure … The music … has neither sentiment, grace, nor vitality." Given the namesake of the Society, these were harsh words.

Some of the premieres occurred at H&H's grand festivals, which began in 1857, and which became triennial after the Civil War. Part of Bach's *St. Matthew Passion* was premiered at the Third Triennial Festival—the *St. Matthew* was performed complete in 1879. Leading Boston critic John Sullivan Dwight called the 1871 *St. Matthew* performance "the highest mark yet reached in the whole history of our Handel and Haydn Society and of choral efforts in this country."

The idea of a festival was first suggested by H&H President Charles Francis Chickering, the son of Jonas Chickering—both of them part of the famed Boston piano manufacturing family. On May 21, 1857, a three-day festival began. The plan, modeled after the Birmingham (England) festivals and maintained for all the later ones, called for an oratorio each night, with various types of afternoon concerts and other occasional events. The afternoon concerts were typically orchestral, with a number of soloists and other offerings. Afternoon audiences heard Beethoven's Fifth and Seventh Symphonies; overtures by Beethoven, Wagner, Rossini, and Mendelssohn; a Vieuxtemps concerto; Weber's *Koncertstück*; and various arias and other solo and small ensemble pieces, including a duet composed for the occasion by the president of the New York American Music Association. The chorus grew to four hundred and fifty, with an orchestra of seventy-eight. The first night, Haydn's *Creation* was performed; the second night, Mendelssohn's *Elijah*; and the festival concluded with Handel's *Messiah*.

In his musical journal, Dwight devoted the bulk of three issues to the event, with analyses and notes on the music and a history of festivals in Europe. Since the 1840s, Dwight, a member of the Transcendentalists, had argued for music that would elevate the listener—music with a spiritual effect, even though it might be secular and instrumental. For him, that meant the classical masters—Haydn, Mozart, and Beethoven—with some allowance for newer composers such as Mendelssohn. In 1853, he continued the fight in his journal for the special recognition of classical music. In his comment on the first H&H festival, Dwight wrote, "Enthusiasm was unbounded … long and loud plaudits shook the hall … for the first time almost in our country has an artistic demonstration here been made, and carried through, upon a grand scale, without false pretence, vain show, or *humbug.*"

The 1857 Music Festival succeeded in every way but financial: tickets brought in $5,336 and expenditures totaled $7,299. A large number of guarantors had subscribed, however, and according to the Society's report, "we have not heard of one

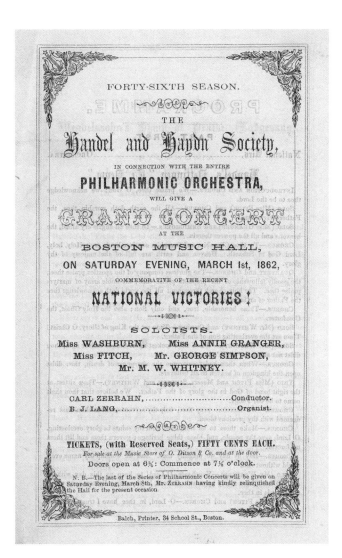

who does not bear the tax [covering the deficit] quite cheerfully; for all regard the Festival as a complete success." In 1862, H&H Secretary Loring B. Barnes proudly noted that the Festival was "the first of the kind ever attempted in this country."

Encouraged, the Society began to plan further festivals, including one in 1859 to commemorate the centenary of Handel's death. With the prospect of a coming national conflict on everyone's mind, however, the idea of another festival was deferred. The Civil War broke out in 1861.

The installation of the great organ in the Boston Music Hall, in 1863, stimulated the Society to again think about an even greater festival, which would combine "all the choral force of the immediate neighborhood of Boston in one great choir." In 1865, as the war was coming to a close, a festival was organized to celebrate the semi-centennial of the Society. A five-day event, it had a chorus of seven hundred and an orchestra of one hundred. Several members of the old Germania Orchestra

LEFT
Program for Handel's *Israel in Egypt*, February 1859

RIGHT
Program for March 1862 concert, "commemorative of the recent National Victories!"

MATTHEW GUERRIERI

SINGING, HYMNBOOKS, AND EDUCATION

IN 1828, Elam Ives, Jr., a church musician and teacher in Berlin, Connecticut, was elected an honorary member of the Handel and Haydn Society. Ives thanked the Society by letter:

> [It is] true, my life has been employed in the cause of Church Music; ... I am fully aware of the importance of my profession, and it is to be regretted that it stands so low ... You are the *fountainhead*, and Teachers are the Channels through which your streams are to flow, and much is yet to be done to prevent the streams from being corrupted.

Music education was part of the H&H mission from the start. In the beginning, its educational efforts were indirect—it was content to be an inspiration, a paragon, a symbol of the fruits of education. Performance came first: the members would demonstrate their musical discrimination by singing works of the most highly regarded composers; the example would prompt listeners to elevate their own taste. Soon after, the Society, for a time, extended its reach via publishing, producing its own collections of approved music, printed wheat to chase out the market's musical chaff. But only after several forestalled attempts would H&H transform itself from being "the fountainhead" of teachers to becoming a teacher itself.

The Society elected its first honorary members in 1816. All, conveniently, were already members of the Society, but two of them would provide examples to spur H&H's first educational efforts. Bartholomew Brown and his brother-in-law, Nahum Mitchell, were lawyers and public servants by trade—Mitchell served a term in Congress and was a longtime judge—but both were also keen musicians. In 1802, the pair produced a book called *Columbian and European Harmony*, better known by

One of H&H's founders, Matthew S. Parker, served as the first secretary, (1815–1819), then as trustee and treasurer until 1866

its second title, the *Bridgewater Collection of Sacred Music*. (The Browns were most likely assisted in the compilation by Benjamin Holt, who would become a founding trustee of the Handel and Haydn Society and its second president.)

The *Bridgewater Collection* became a best-seller, going through multiple editions. An oft-cited figure claimed more than one hundred thousand copies sold. The fourth edition, published in 1816 under the more solemn title *Templi Carmina*, "Songs of the Temple," carried a testimonial from Matthew S. Parker, the secretary of the Handel and Haydn Society. By 1820, the collection was in its eighth edition, a copy of which was acquired by a bank teller in Savannah, Georgia, named Lowell Mason.

Born in Medfield, Massachusetts, in 1792, Mason was the eldest of five children of Johnson and Catherine Mason. The family was middle-class, prosperous, upstanding. Johnson Mason was a merchant and a frequent holder of various municipal offices. Catherine was a devout churchgoer who requested of her husband that he keep his theological doubts to himself for the sake of the children.

Lowell grew up surrounded by music. Both his parents were members of the church choir, and his father also occasionally played the double bass. Lowell studied with a myriad of local teachers, among them Amos Albee, who had published his own tune book, the *Norfolk Collection of Church Music*, and Oliver Shaw, a blind composer in nearby Dedham who, in later life, would become a best-selling songwriter—"There's Nothing True But Heaven," to a poem by Thomas Moore, was a bona fide hit. (Shaw had himself studied with Gottlieb Graupner, who would go on to help found H&H.)

By the time he was sixteen, Lowell Mason was directing the local church choir, but his father tried to discourage a musical career. It was Johnson Mason who encouraged

OPPOSITE
Lowell Mason
in his study

his son—who had "spent twenty years of his life in doing nothing save playing upon all manner of instruments that came within his reach"—to relocate to Savannah and establish himself in some other occupation. The father's objections to a musical profession were not just financial, but moral. "[Y]ou will find plenty of Wolves in Sheaps Clothing," he warned Lowell on the eve of his departure (and with idiosyncratic spelling), "especially in the [s]cience of Music for that will probably make your circle of acquaintance large in a short space of time so there will not be that chance to distinguish the real characters of your acquaintance that there would be in some other occupations." The musician's life was a gateway to—literally—the dangers of fast living.

Nevertheless, upon his arrival in Savannah, Mason promptly began to multitask. He opened a singing school, enrolling some thirty students in a course of sacred music ("this delightful and useful accomplishment," as an advertisement assured). Within a couple of years, he once again became a choir director, at Savannah's Independent Presbyterian Church, and eventually added the position of organist. He continued studying, now with Frederick Abel, who had emigrated to Savannah in 1817, fully versed in "scientific" European musical practice. (Abel's uncle, Carl Frederick Abel, was a student of J. S. Bach and later became a musical celebrity in London, collaborating with one of Bach's sons.)

With Abel's help, Mason began compiling a hymnbook of his own. The connection to Europe was more than incidental. In his choice of tunes and the dos and don'ts of getting from chord to chord, Mason was deliberately trying to be more in line with European, rather than American, practice. One of Mason's main sources for his collection was a collection by the English composer William Gardiner; the title of Gardiner's book, *Sacred Melodies, from Haydn, Mozart and Beethoven, Adapted to the Best English Poets, and Appropriated to the Use of the British Church*, advertised its provenance. Gardiner had wished only to rescue passing bits of melody that caught his ear in the works of those masters. Mason's intention, though, was to rescue American church music itself.

It was an intention that could have been designed to appeal to the newly formed Handel and Haydn Society. The Society's Act of Incorporation spoke of "extending the knowledge and improving the style of performance of Church music," and also complained that "the admirers of music find their beloved science far from exciting the feelings or exercising the powers to which it is accustomed in the Old World." The problem, to their ears, was that American composers had taken independence too far.

To judge from contemporary commentary, no one had epitomized that excess independence as much as Boston's William Billings (1746–1800). A tanner by trade,

THE

BOSTON HANDEL AND HAYDN SOCIETY COLLECTION

OF

SACRED MUSIC,

CONSISTING OF

SONGS, DUETTS, TRIOS, CHORUSSES, ANTHEMS, &c.

SELECTED FROM THE WORKS OF THE MOST CELEBRATED AUTHORS.

ARRANGED FOR THE ORGAN OR PIANO FORTE.

BY THE

HANDEL AND HAYDN SOCIETY.

Vol. I.

———

BOSTON :

PUBLISHED BY THE HANDEL AND HAYDN SOCIETY,

THOMAS BADGER, Jr. PRINTER.

1821.

The Boston Handel and Haydn Society Collection of Sacred Music, 1821. This copy was signed "John H. Pray, 1822." John H. Pray joined H&H on July 6, 1815.

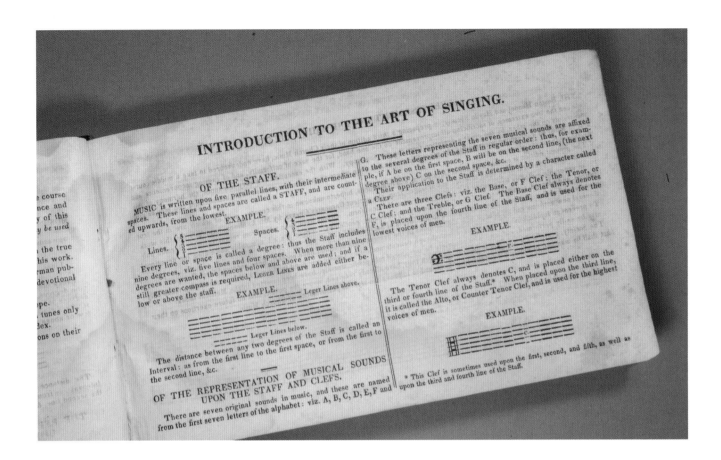

The Boston Handel
and Haydn Society
Collection of
Church Music,
1822

self-taught in music, and notorious for his eccentricities (which were invariably cited by his critics), Billings was, nonetheless, the first significant native-born American composer. In between a potpourri of careers (for a time he was the city's hogreeve, responsible for rounding up and impounding loose pigs), he published six collections of anthems and hymn tunes. His music was bright, busy, rhythmically robust, and cheerfully indifferent to the niceties of learned European counterpoint. In time, Billings' genius would come to be celebrated; in the early years of the Handel and Haydn Society, it was to be shunned, plowed under, decried with moral fervor as crude and unscientific. (The reaction went both ways. Some who felt that the reformers were excessively censorious in their rejection of the older music founded their own organization—the Billings and Holden Society—and published their own collection of *Ancient Psalmody*.)

Faced with a deluge of unacceptable hymnbooks and collections—Billings and his publications were only the most prominent in a corps of colonial hymnodists—the Handel and Haydn Society decided to get into the publishing game itself. Early on, it had partnered with the Old Colony Musical Society (led by none other than Bartholomew Brown) to produce the *Old Colony Collection of Anthems*, a compendium of choral works by (mostly) European composers. Editorial control of later volumes of the *Old Colony Collection* was completely taken over by H&H, and *The Boston Handel and Haydn Society Collection of Sacred Music*, a collection of oratorio excerpts, followed in 1821.

So when, having unsuccessfully shopped the manuscript to publishers in Philadelphia and Boston, Mason brought his project to the Society's attention, it must have seemed tailor-made for the burgeoning Handel and Haydn brand—a book of everyday church repertoire to complement the Society's other collections of choral showpieces. However, despite the intention and Mason's nascent reputation—one of his arrangements had even been accepted for the second volume of the *Old Colony Collection*—H&H decided that the hymnbook would first have to pass muster with some kind of authority. So it turned to the biggest authority in Boston at the time.

For a few years, Dr. George K. Jackson loomed large in Boston's musical life, both figuratively and literally—he reportedly weighed at least three hundred pounds. An organist and composer, he emigrated from England in time to lose a job for refusing to swear allegiance to the United States after the outbreak of the War of 1812. The Society sought his services for its early concerts, but Jackson asked for so much money that it turned out to be cheaper to import an organist from New York.

Still, Jackson's approval was valuable enough that the Society approached him regarding the new hymnbook. Mason, who had traveled back to Boston in search of a publisher, duly scheduled a series of meetings with Jackson to go over the materials. Mason agreed to add a few of Jackson's own compositions, and Jackson vouchsafed his blessing; *The Boston Handel and Haydn Society Collection of Church Music*, "Being a Selection of the Most Approved Psalm and Hymn Tunes; Together with Many Beautiful Extracts from the Works of Haydn, Mozart, Beethoven, and Other Eminent Modern Composers," was published by the Boston firm of Richardson and Lord in 1822.

The collection was successful beyond anyone's expectation. Over the next two decades it went through twenty-two editions and become a standard in churches throughout the country. In its style, following European rules, it solidified the Society's reputation for musical propriety ("The public taste is rapidly improving," Elam Ives assured H&H members.) It established Mason's reputation to the point at which, in later editions, his name would go from a passing mention in the preface to a prominent place on the title page. It had the honor of being pirated. It made, not incidentally, Mason and H&H an enormous amount of money—at least $10,000 each in royalties. The survival of the Society—even as a number of similar organizations in other cities that followed in its wake foundered—owed much to the steady influx of cash from the book.

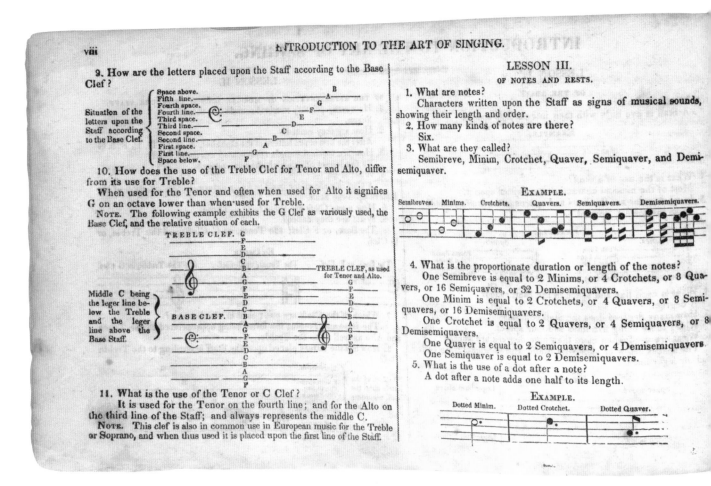

The Boston Handel and Haydn Society Collection of Church Music, 13th edition, 1833

Mason returned to Savannah, but his ambition was now directed north. Much later, he would recall walking along the Savannah River and seeing a ship headed for Boston. "How I wish I was going to Boston on that schooner," Mason said to himself, "to be made president of the Handel and Haydn Society."

He realized that dream in 1827. The previous year, Mason had again visited Boston, this time giving a well-received lecture on the necessity and prospects for reforming church music. A group of Bostonians was impressed enough to form a committee to try to convince Mason to return to Massachusetts permanently. Mason turned down all the offers—but reversed his decision when, it seems, informal word reached him that the presidency of the Handel and Haydn Society would soon be vacant, and that it might be his if he wanted it. He packed up and moved his family back to Boston, where he would live until 1851.

He would remain president of H&H for only five seasons, however. At the time, it was the president who was responsible for rehearsing and conducting the concerts.

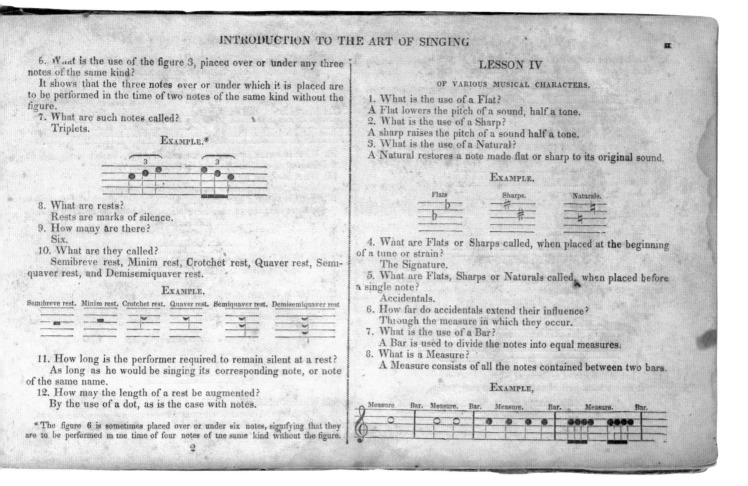

6. What is the use of the figure 3, placed over or under any three notes of the same kind?

It shows that the three notes over or under which it is placed are to be performed in the time of two notes of the same kind without the figure.

7. What are such notes called?

Triplets.

EXAMPLE.*

8. What are rests?

Rests are marks of silence.

9. How many are there?

Six.

10. What are they called?

Semibreve rest, Minim rest, Crotchet rest, Quaver rest, Semiquaver rest, and Demisemiquaver rest.

EXAMPLE.

Semibreve rest. Minim rest. Crotchet rest. Quaver rest. Semiquaver rest. Demisemiquaver rest.

11. How long is the performer required to remain silent at a rest?

As long as he would be singing its corresponding note, or note of the same name.

12. How may the length of a rest be augmented?

By the use of a dot, as is the case with notes.

*The figure 6 is sometimes placed over or under six notes, signifying that they are to be performed in the time of four notes of the same kind without the figure.

2

LESSON IV

OF VARIOUS MUSICAL CHARACTERS.

1. What is the use of a Flat?

A Flat lowers the pitch of a sound, half a tone.

2. What is the use of a Sharp?

A sharp raises the pitch of a sound half a tone.

3. What is the use of a Natural?

A Natural restores a note made flat or sharp to its original sound.

EXAMPLE.

Flats   Sharps.   Naturals.

4. What are Flats or Sharps called, when placed at the beginning of a tune or strain?

The Signature.

5. What are Flats, Sharps or Naturals called, when placed before a single note?

Accidentals.

6. How far do accidentals extend their influence?

Through the measure in which they occur.

7. What is the use of a Bar?

A Bar is used to divide the notes into equal measures.

8. What is a Measure?

A Measure consists of all the notes contained between two bars.

EXAMPLE,

Measure   Bar.   Measure.   Bar.   Measure.   Bar.   Measure.   Bar.

The Board eventually gave Mason *carte blanche* in programming as well, but the concert receipts remained stagnant, even as publishing revenues continued to grow. The symbiosis between Mason and H&H continued to flourish; *The Boston Handel and Haydn Society Collection of Church Music* was still selling well and, by the end of his tenure, Mason would produce another collection, *The Choir, or Union Collection of Church Music*, in 1832. But there is some evidence that Mason found H&H itself a little too democratic for his tastes. His replacement of Sophia Ostinelli as the Society's organist with the German-trained Charles Zeuner resulted in a letter of protest from thirty-eight members; the decision was upheld only by a narrowly divided Board of Trustees.

In the meantime, Mason had started his own informal singing school for children. This brought him to the attention of William Woodbridge, a Yale-educated teacher who had become a convert to the ideas of the Swiss educational reformer Johann Heinrich Pestalozzi. Pestalozzi prescribed incremental, experiential learning in place of rote memorization; a Swiss composer named Hans Georg Nägeli translated Pestalozzi's ideas into a method for teaching music. (Nägeli's method was, in turn, translated into English by Elam Ives, who had been another target of Woodbridge's proselytizing.) Woodbridge cultivated Mason, who, intrigued by Nägeli's curriculum, began to devote more and more energy to the idea of children's education. As a result, the year after he left the H&H presidency, Mason founded the Boston Academy of Music, with the intent of promoting a Pestalozzian system of music education.

The Academy had enough connections to the Handel and Haydn Society to be considered, on paper, an ally of a sort; of particular importance was George J. Webb, an English organist and composer who had arrived in Boston in 1830, promptly joining H&H and beginning a collaboration with Mason in his singing-school efforts. While the nominal leadership of the Boston Academy would be filled by a parade of public-minded eminences—the most prominent being Samuel A. Eliot, congressman and later mayor of Boston—it was Mason who was the driving force, Mason and Webb who taught most of the Academy's classes, and Mason who presided over the Academy's most lasting educational achievement, the addition of music to Boston Public Schools. The Academy had petitioned the school board to let it shepherd a pilot program; when the city council dropped the matter, Mason went ahead and did it anyway.

Mason, of course, continued to publish. *The Boston Academy's Collection of Church Music* came out in 1835, but its success was qualified, at least by those in H&H who felt that Mason had made too free use of his work in the Society's published collections. Resentment of Mason's success had previously been tamped down, but the founding of the Boston Academy and the publication of *The Boston Academy's Collection* brought the rancor to the surface. A memorandum in the Society archives preserves the grumbling in unusually pristine form. The author is unknown (George Washington Lucas, a Society member and outspoken Mason critic, would make a plausible suspect), but the accusation is clear: Mason had defrauded the Society both musically and financially:

> Mr. Mason was not considered *entirely* competent to make a *correct* book; so that, when the H.&H. Society had taken from him his book in manuscript and had agreed to adopt it as their own,—they first took it to Doctor Jackson, and by *him* it was revised & corrected.

> It was afterwards ... thoroughly revised by Mr. Zeuner, who took and stripped the tunes, & re-wrote all but the melodies ... Mr. Mason used to speak of Zeuner's alterations and amendments of the tunes in the H.&H. Collection, as of *great value*; and the free use he has made of them, in several of his later publications, is proof of his sincerity, in so speaking.

Choir practice at the High School of Commerce, Boston, in the 1890s

Mr. Mason's dealings with the Society were not suspected of being unfair until the evidence of it was too late found in Contract no. 3 dated 1832. Prior to that time he had withdrawn from the Society & had established the Academy of Music. The Choir was compiled by him, soon after he left the H.&H.S.—and next followed the Academy Collection. That book has superseded ours having been manufactured in part out of our materials … and the H.&H. Society Collection is now scarcely used at all.

The rumors and accusations eventually reached Mason's ears; he suggested that a report "made to the [Society] would probably have a tendency to enlighten those who are now ignorant on the subject." The ignorance may have been of the fact that H&H still had a financial interest in Mason's subsequent publications. Repeatedly, money would spark friction between the Society and its illustrious ex-president; repeatedly, money would smooth things over. Still, by the early 1840s, the contracts with Mason were dissolved. Mason and the Handel and Haydn Society continued to make respectful reference to each other—graciously citing their one-time connection—but the connection was done.

Just after the Boston Academy's founding, a committee of trustees, led by H&H President Charles Lovett and Vice President Jonas Chickering, was formed to consider whether the Society should follow suit. Their report, issued around 1835, established the groundwork for a Handel and Haydn Academy of Music. Charles Zeuner, the Society's organist, was to be the instructor; classes would meet once a week for a six-month term. The proposed regulations give some hint of the turf war simmering between the Academy and the Society, with the Society's students required to pledge "to assist no other public Musical Institution, either by rehearsal or Concerts." In spite of its high-level advocacy, the H&H Academy seems to have never gotten off the ground.

The idea of the H&H Academy may have fallen victim to a leadership shuffle around the same time—Bartholomew Brown, the editor of the *Bridgewater Collection*, was elected president for the 1836–1837 season, only to leave abruptly and form a rival institution, the Musical Institute of Boston (along with Nahum Mitchell and Louis Ostinelli, who had often served as concertmaster for Society performances and whose wife had been let go as the Society's organist by Mason). At the same time, friction developed between Mason and Webb, to the point of some sort of falling out and, in late 1839, Webb resigned from the Boston Academy.

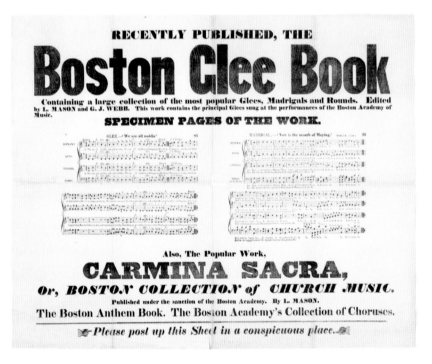

Advertisement for two songbooks associated with the Boston Academy of Music founded by Lowell Mason in 1833

ORDER OF EXERCISES

IN THE HANDEL AND HAYDN SOCIETY'S
ANNUAL COURSE OF MUSICAL INSTRUCTION.

Hours.	Tuesday. Aug. 17th.	Wednes'y. 18th.	Thursday, 19th.	Friday, 20th.	Saturday, 21st.	Monday, 23d.	Tuesday, 24th.	Wednes'y. 25th.	Thursday, 26th.	Friday, 27th.
8 to 9.		Lecture on Elementary Teaching, J.F Warner.	"	"	"	"	"	"	"	"
9 to 10.		Practice of Psalmody, &c G. J. Webb.	"	"	"	"	"	"	"	"
10 to 11.	Lecture on Elementary Teaching. J.F.Warner	Lecture on Harmony G. J. Webb.	"	"	"	"	"	"	"	"
11 to 12.	Practice on Psalmody & Chanting. G. J. Webb		Convention.	"	"	"	"	"	"	"
12 to 1.	Lecture on Harmony. G. J. Webb.		Convention.	"	"	"	"	"	"	"
3 to 4.	Glee Singing G. J. Webb	"	Lecture on Æsthetics J. F.Warner	"	"	"	Lecture on the Piano-forte. H. Greatorex	Lecture by Mr Hayward	Lecture on Instruments. G J. Webb.	
4 to 5.	Lecture on the Voice. H Greatorex	"	✕	"	Solo Singing H Greatorex.	"	"	"	Lecture by Mr Hayward	
7½	Chorus Singing. G. J. Webb.	"	Glee Singing G. J. Webb.	Chorus Singing G. J. Webb.	Oratorio of Mount Sinai. By the H. & H. Soc.	Glee Singing G. J. Webb	Chorus Singing G. J. Webb	Social Concert.	Lecture on the Organ. H. Greatorex	

The performance of Handel's Messiah by H. & H. Society, Sunday Evening, Aug. 22.

Butts, Printer, 2 School St.

Webb was promptly elected, once again, president of the Handel and Haydn Society, and, by 1841, was eyeing the National Musical Convention, started by Mason and his Academy, as an opportunity for H&H. He proposed that the Society offer its own class, concurrent with the Musical Convention, for "such Ladies and Gentlemen as are in some degree familiar with the principles of reading music, and are desirous of cultivating the higher beauties of the art." That put the Society and the Academy in direct competition. A scheduled Convention debate ("Do oratorios, as they are generally conducted, exert a salutary influence in the cause of church music?") was taken by Society supporters as an attack, and the Convention dissolved. Mason's adherents broke off and formed their own gathering—the American Musical Convention—but the divide caused both conventions to dissolve within a few years. The Handel and Haydn classes, needless to say, were not repeated.

The discord apparently scared the Society away from one of Webb's other ideas, this one for a full-scale, full-time school. Webb's proposed Boston Handel and Haydn Society's Conservatory of Music was ambitious in scope: a full curriculum, twenty to forty weeks of classes each year, permanent professors. The project was "reported on favorably," but then abandoned, after Webb's over-aggressive promotion rankled other Society officials. Webb declined re-nomination for the H&H presidency the following season. He soon made amends with Lowell Mason, and their renewed professional association lasted until Mason's retirement; Webb's daughter married Mason's

OPPOSITE
Program for
Mendelssohn's
Elijah, December
1854, with soloists
from the Solo
School, one of
several H&H
programs designed
to train solo singers

son. (Webb nonetheless left a souvenir of their dispute, in the form of a void: his own H&H-sponsored hymnbook, *The Massachusetts Collection of Psalmody*, published in 1840—in the midst of the falling out—contained none of Mason's compositions.)

The conservatory idea was resurrected in 1854, when Josiah Fairbanks, the Society's secretary (he would soon be elected president, serving in that office for a single season) suggested forming a Handel and Haydn Society Solo School, meeting in the summer, open by audition to members of the Society ("and such ladies as the Board of Trustees may invite"). The Solo School had more seeming wherewithal than the Society's previous efforts: some thirty-five students were enrolled; Arthur Arthurson, an English tenor who performed often with the Society, and F. F. Mueller, the Society's organist, were chosen as instructors; a set of Regulations and Conditions was handsomely printed up. Like the abandoned Handel and Haydn Academy, the Regulations included a pledge of allegiance from members to "render such *aid* and *service* at the Winter Concerts and Rehearsals of the Society as may be required of them during the year."

Such aid and service were provided during the following season: students from the Solo School took numerous solo roles in the Society's performance of Mendelssohn's *Elijah*. The experiment seems to have been only an equivocal success, and the school closed down after a single term. The roll book goes blank after four classes; any other mention of the school disappears after only a few months more. The Society's two previous attempts at hands-on education had at least ended in small outbursts of acrimonious closure. The Solo School seems to have just faded away.

By the time it lent its voices to the opening of the National Education Association Exercises, held in Boston in July 1910, the Society was a pendant, a once-removed cousin to the public-school efforts that originated with Lowell Mason. At the Exercises, the Association paid due tribute to Mason and, in the process, to itself. Mason had moved to New York City in 1851, and retired to New Jersey in 1860, where he died twelve years later, but Boston was still eager to claim some of his luster and legacy. Leonard B. Marshall, assistant director of music for the Boston Public Schools, was certain that, "If Lowell Mason could return to this world and witness the great progress which has been made in his chosen art … how gratified would he be and how thankful that he had been instrumental in initiating the glorious work." It was left to another assistant director, Grant Drake, to sound a lone dissenting note: "I sometimes fear we confound *talking* about success with the thing itself," he warned. "They are quite different."

To the Handel and Haydn Society's credit, it would now and again move beyond talk. In 1924 and 1925, the Society mounted concerts for schoolchildren, with

ORATORIO

OF

ELIJAH:

BY MENDELSSOHN, (OP. 70.)

WILL BE PERFORMED BY THE

Handel and Haydn Society,

BEING THE FIRST OF THE SERIES OF EIGHT CONCERTS,

ON SUNDAY EVENING, DECEMBER 3, 1854,

AT THE BOSTON MUSIC HALL,

ASSISTED BY

Mr. H. M. AIKEN, (as Elijah).	. . . . .	Basso.
" A. ARTHURSON,	. . . . . .	Tenor.

BY THE FOLLOWING MEMBERS OF THE SOCIETY'S SOLO CLASS:

Mrs. F. A. HILL.	Miss HESSELTINE.	Messrs. G. H. CONEY.
" S. MESTON.	" TWICHELL.	" J. P. DRAPER.
" S. F. WOOD.	" IDE.	" G. GOVE.
	" LEACH.	" W. B. BOTHAMLY.

AND THE ORCHESTRAL UNION.

FIRST VIOLIN,	. . . .	SHULTZE, A. FRIES, MEISEL & SUCK.	
SECOND "	. . . .	HEHL, FRENZEL, EICHLER & GROVES.	
TENORS	. . . .	KREBS, RYAN & SCHLIMPER.	
VIOLONCELLOS	. W. FRIES & MAAS.	BASSOONS	THIEDE & HUNSTOCK.
CONTRA BASSOS	BALKE & REGESTEIN.	HORNS	HAMANN & RUDOLPHSEN.
FLUTES	ZOHLER & RAMETTI.	TRUMPETS	HEINEKE & PINTER.
OBOES	RIBAS & FAHRWASSER.	TROMBONES	RIMBACH, REGESTEIN & STEIN.
CLARIONETS	SHULTZ & McDONALD.	TYMPANI	STOHR.

Conductor.	- - -	Mr. CARL ZERRAHN.
Organist,	- - -	" F. F. MÜLLER.

reduced-fare tickets (35¢, a slight premium on the 25¢ movie tickets of the day) and programs of excerpts from standard H&H fare: *Messiah*, *Elijah*, Verdi's Requiem. The first concert was given without an orchestra and just about broke even; the second added an orchestra, and the resulting financial loss was enough to scuttle the effort after only two seasons.

Thompson Stone, the Society's director from 1927 to 1959, made a point of involving school-age singers as participants rather than merely passive listeners. His numerous performances of Bach's *St. Matthew Passion* invariably featured local (and, occasionally, visiting) boys' choirs for selected chorales, and, in 1938, a citywide, two-hundred-voice children's chorus was assembled for performances of Gabriel Pierné's *Children's Crusade*. The choir, rehearsed by H&H organist William Burbank, also music director for Brookline Public Schools, attracted a fair amount of press attention, but, after the interruption of World War II, such large-scale collaborations disappeared. Educational efforts retreated to an annual Young People's *Messiah* concert.

In the early 1960s, in advance of its 150th anniversary, H&H commissioned a Survey and Planning Report from the Boston-based public relations firm Newsome &

OFFICIAL PROGRAM

Music For The People · By The People
Boston's First Music Week
MAY · 4 ·· 10 · 1924

Music Knows NO RACE NOR CREED

Company. As might be expected, the report was laced with pragmatic strategies for getting the Society's name and image before the public—the school-aged public included. The report suggested, for instance, an H&H-sponsored high school choral festival. It also mentioned, almost as a passing brainstorm, the formation of a Junior Handel and Haydn Society: "A Junior Society (up to 13 or 14 years in age) could be rehearsed and could perform works completely separate from the Society, or it could be rehearsed to perform one concert yearly with the parent Society—or both."

The hypothetical expansions of H&H's youth programs were not only designed to expand the audience, but also to follow the money. "Since it seems doubtful that many foundations would contribute to the costs of the 150th Anniversary Celebration itself," the report noted, "the selling point to the majority of the foundations should be the Society's youth program." It would take another twenty-five years, but that combination—audience-building, community involvement, and fundraising possibilities—would prompt the Society's most involved educational undertaking since the short-lived 1854 Solo School.

olor Sketch based on Architects' Drawing of the Washington Cathedral, as it will be seen from the Southeast when com

PIERNÉ'S
Children's Crusade

PRESENTED BY THE

HANDEL and HAYDN
SOCIETY
SYMPHONIC CHORUS OF 300 VOICES

Dr. THOMPSON STONE, Conductor

AGNES DAVIS	BLANCHE HASKELL	OLIVE APPLETON
Soprano	*Soprano*	*Soprano*

ERNEST McCHESNEY	WALTER KIDDER
Tenor	*Bass*

CHILDREN'S CHORUS OF 200 VOICES
he BROOKLINE PUBLIC SCHOOLS   *Trained by* WILLIAM B. BURBA

YMPHONY HALL	SEVENTY-SEVEN MEMBERS OF THE Boston	MONDAY OCT. 31

H&H Vocal
Quartet members
David Howse, bass;
Yukiko Ueno, piano;
Heather Holland,
alto; Susan Consoli,
soprano; Samuel
Martinborough,
tenor, 2002

Style was the priority when Thomas Dunn took over as artistic director in 1967. Dunn ambitiously remade H&H into an ensemble and chorus dedicated to historically informed performance; education was a secondary concern. In 1986, Dunn gave a valedictory presentation to the Board of Governors, outlining his recommendations for the Society's future. The title was "The Artistic Crisis Facing the H&H." It contained no mention of education.

Still, there was recognition within H&H that some kind of educational initiative might be vital to the Society's long-term survival. Occasional proposals for school outreach were drawn up and considered; one specified that the objective was "to penetrate the barriers and apprehension that many people have about the classical forms of music … to rebuild an audience for classical." Around the end of Dunn's tenure, such an outreach program had been launched: a quintet of H&H chorus members, along with a pianist, was sent out to junior high and high schools, presenting short programs and answering questions. It was a modest start.

The next music director, Christopher Hogwood, was more of an advocate for education. "I'd like to do even more [outreach]," Hogwood announced soon after his appointment. "There is much enthusiasm for H&H once the public has had the opportunity to taste of its offerings." His enthusiasm eventually evolved into a grand if speculative vision for H&H education programs. Outlining his hopes for development, Hogwood proposed, in 1991, that within the next decade, the Society should produce its own television series ("It's difficult to fully describe this series," he said, "but the closest analogy would be the Bernstein *Young People's Concerts* of the 1950s and '60s"), as well as a series of educational videos for use in schools. That never came to pass, but Hogwood's prodding did result in a crucial expansion of the education program.

Outreach concerts, to begin with, became participatory affairs: school choruses prepared repertoire that they would then perform in tandem with members of the chorus and orchestra. Shepherding the effort was the Society's new assistant director, Jeffrey Rink. (The H&H job was the start of a long career in Boston for Rink, who would go on to conduct both the New England Philharmonic and Chorus pro Musica for many years.) At the first of these concerts, at Faneuil Hall in March 1987, members of public high school choruses from Cambridge, Malden, and New Bedford—each having been coached by Rink—joined the H&H Educational Ensemble (now up to a sextet) to sing Handel's Coronation Anthem *Let thy hand be strengthened*. The following season, four choruses sang in a performance of Vivaldi's Gloria. In the spring of 1988, five school choruses combined to join H&H members in Brahms' *Liebeslieder Waltzes* and selections from Vaughan Williams' *Folk Songs of the Four Seasons* in a concert at Lowell High School. "We try to break down the barrier to show them that this is an art form open to all of them," Rink explained in an interview published in *The Christian Science Monitor*. "It's not some sort of indoor sport where they go and just 'spectate.' They're able through supervision and assistance to

Christopher Hogwood and audience members after an outreach concert by the Boston Composers' String Quartet at Lewis Middle School, Roxbury, 1995

create something quite extraordinary—far beyond what many people feel they're capable of." The Society's longstanding habit of educating solely by example was being broken.

But just as the new, and newly named, Collaborative Youth Concerts were expanding, the outreach program had a moment of financial reckoning. The indirect cause was the failure of hundreds of American savings and loan institutions; the S&L crisis of the late 1980s fueled a recession that quickly trickled down to the arts. In 1989, the Massachusetts Council on the Arts and Humanities saw its budget cut by forty-five percent; among the casualties was an annual $40,000 to fund H&H outreach activities. In response, the H&H Board not only made moves to cover the shortfall, shifting $25,000 to the education budget, but also decided to put education on organizational par with concerts and recordings, voting, in October 1990, "to make Educational Outreach a core activity, no longer a special project."

As it happened, education was about to be H&H's main tool for attacking a long-standing and, at the same time, newly pressing problem. "Handel & Haydn: Diversity is Elusive," *The Boston Globe* announced via headline; the January 1991 article, by Diane Lewis and Patti Hartigan, spelled out what the headline summed up: "Of the 38 members on the governing board, 37 are white and one is Asian. Of the 30 to 35 young professional singers who make up Handel & Haydn's chorus, one is black and one is Hispanic. And the eight singers and two pianists who make up the society's education-outreach program are all white."

Diversity had been stymied for multiple reasons. On the artistic side, the move to period-practice performance, started under Dunn, had accelerated under Hogwood, and the period-practice performance world, from which the Society might recruit and hire, was still relatively small, insular, and not particularly diverse. H&H's Board had formed an Affirmative Action Committee, but the committee stalled, falling through

Collaborative Youth Concert conducted by John Finney with members of the Period Instrument Orchestra, 2007

the cracks of Board turnover. The education program had continued—and predominantly minority-attended schools remained the priority for visits and youth concerts—but the program's very existence was symptomatic of the steady erosion of arts education in public schools, particularly those in minority neighborhoods. The meager pool of minority musicians that the Society might have drawn on was not getting any bigger. Underserved students with musical talent were not getting the early engagement with Baroque and Classical music that would allow their talent to develop into the stylistic expertise around which the Society had reoriented its artistic mission.

The growing sense was that the H&H educational mission needed to become even more proactive. The result was the Vocal Apprenticeship Program—individual lessons for talented high-school-aged singers, organized and paid for by the Society, along with a chorus, the "Junior Handel and Haydn Society" idea floated in the 1960s now made into a practical vehicle for teaching music literacy. The hope was that students in the program would also be role models at their own schools; the program would depend in part on teachers and administrators in the schools to help identify promising students and promote the idea. But the idea marked a turning point: the Society would soon organize its own independent, hands-on educational efforts, seeding talent and enthusiasm for the future.

Though the proposal was prompt—drafts of plans for the Vocal Apprenticeship Program, today the Vocal Arts Program, were circulating by the spring of 1991—H&H itself would need to call on educational talent in order to get VAP, as the program became known, off the ground. The program was unprecedented for the Society, but not the first of its kind in Boston: since 1982 the Boston Symphony Orchestra had been offering its own program of instrumental instruction for black and Latino students, called Project STEP. H&H would draw on that experience when, in 1993, Barbara E. Maze, Project STEP's former president, joined the H&H Board of Governors. The Society already had a number of board members advocating strongly for education—Janet Whitla (who had also served as president of the U.S. Coalition for Education in Art), Karen Levy, and Candace Achtmeyer. Maze had the complementary advantage of practical experience.

Accomplishment was a custom for Maze. One of her first jobs was at Filene's, the Boston department store, where she became the store's first African-American buyer, after having the audacity and self-confidence to ask to be considered for the position. Widowed at a young age, she raised a daughter on her own. She was admitted to Boston University, but left before graduating; later in life, she would return, earn a master's degree, and eventually become BU's assistant dean for student affairs. She had a graceful manner wrapped around a steely core. Difficulties, for Maze, were opportunities.

Education Committee members Eugene Grant, Kathleen Weld, Julian Bullitt, Candace Achtmeyer, and Karen Levy surround Robin Baker, Barbara Maze, and Maze Award recipient Nicole Ameduri, June 13, 1998

Maze had a passion for music. An enthusiastic singer, she brought to the Society a zeal for ensuring that students might have the kind of musical opportunities she had lacked. Maze, along with Robin Lee Baker—the Society's new director of education, promoted from her previous position as the organization's administrative coordinator and later archivist—began to remake the education program from the ground up. Baker undertook a year of research into curricula, funding sources, and facilities. At the outset, her brief included a variety of efforts: not only the existing school collaborations, but also pre-concert lectures, a particular interest of Hogwood's; a slate of historically focused concerts, in collaboration with the Boston Composers' String Quartet; and a multicultural chamber series, curated with input from H&H chorus and orchestra members. But the education program eventually became focused on renewing and expanding the Society's outreach to the young.

Even language came under scrutiny. The outreach program had continued to expand—enthusiasm on the part of teachers in the visited schools was strong—but a certain ad hoc approach to programming sometimes led to communication failures: on one school visit, an H&H singer asked a roomful of inner-city students if any of them had ever been on a fox hunt. Scripts and programs for the school-outreach ensembles were rewritten and retooled.

The first VAP ensemble, Youth Chorus, for middle-school students, provided basic instruction and performance experience; the High School Soloists, twelve every year, received individual instruction and counsel in both technique and preparation for higher education in music. Twenty-seven students were auditioned and enrolled in Youth Chorus the first year; *Boston Globe* music critic Richard Dyer paid notice to the inaugural VAP concert, in June 1994: "For these singers, and for the Vocal Apprenticeship Program, this concert was a tentative first step, but no step in the direction of music is a false step."

Dyer did not gloss over the circumstances driving VAP. "One remembered regretfully that 40 years ago even small towns in Oklahoma had school choruses that sang this literature; today the Athens of America does not," he wrote. "These youngsters are lucky, and one felt sorry for all their classmates who will never have this experience." As the vacuum in public-school arts education expanded, VAP expanded as well. The H&H Treble Ensemble (later renamed the Young Women's Chorus) started in 1998 under the direction of Sandra Piques Eddy, who would later join the roster of The Metropolitan Opera. (According to Baker, one of the catalysts for the creation of the Young Women's Chorus was a reluctance on the part of the Society to choose between Eddy and Doralene Davis, who had both applied to direct the Youth Chorus; a second ensemble allowed H&H to hire both.) Matthew Garrett, a versatile choral conductor and clinician who joined the H&H staff in 1999, helmed further expansion of the program. The H&H Singers, for elementary school students, began under Garrett's direction in 1999. He also laid the groundwork for a male

Vocal Arts Program Soloists

LEFT
Deborah Pierre

CENTER
Demeyer Lauture, Jr.

RIGHT
Evangelyna Etienne

counterpart to the high-school-age Young Women's Chorus; the Young Men's Chorus made its debut in 2006, with Joseph Stillitano conducting.

The Education Program, as its growth accelerated, went from a secondary effort to a primary activity of the Society. Supporting the program became the focus of most of the Society's fundraising, and VAP became an increasingly visible part of its main concert series. The Young Women's Chorus and Young Men's Chorus joined the H&H Chorus and Orchestra for Holiday Sing programs at Symphony Hall in 2006 and 2007, respectively; both would return to the Symphony Hall stage in 2012, with Harry Christophers conducting, to sing (shades of Thompson Stone) chorales in Bach's *St. Matthew Passion*. The Youth Chorus had made its Symphony Hall debut in 1999, in the Society's world-premiere performances of Dan Welcher's oratorio, *JFK: The Voice of Peace*. That was indicative also of how much education became an impetus for the Society's involvement in new music; almost all the Society's premieres since the 1980s have involved its education program.

As the Handel and Haydn Society's Bicentennial approached, the Education Program had grown to the point of reaching thousands of students each year: a dozen

OPPOSITE
Young Men's Chorus,
2013

ABOVE
Young Women's
Chorus with
conductor Lisa
Graham, 2006

ABOVE
Guest Conductor Bernard
Labadie and H&H/New
England Conservatory
Conductor Apprentice
Joshua Weilerstein.
Established in 2010,
this program gives
young conductors the
opportunity to work with
leaders in historically
informed performance.

OPPOSITE
H&H Vocal Quartet
1991–2013

pre-college singers being mentored as High School Soloists and over one hundred students meeting every Saturday for rehearsals for the newly named Vocal Arts Program choruses, along with theory and sight-singing classes. Another three hundred students from various school districts participated in the Collaborative Youth Concerts, which had continued and thrived, after Jeffrey Rink's departure, under H&H Assistant Conductor and Chorusmaster John Finney, and had become something approaching annual tradition at many of the participating schools. The educational ensemble—now a specially hired quartet of professional singers, plus a pianist—was traveling to thirty-one schools in nine cities across eastern Massachusetts. In however roundabout and modernized a way, H&H had resurrected an old idea: the Society had created its own academy.

On May 22, 2011, the Handel and Haydn Society Young Men's Chorus participated in a concert in Medfield, Massachusetts. The concert commemorated the relocation of Lowell Mason's birthplace. The house had been in danger of demolition by developers; through Lowell Mason, Medfield was reclaiming a favorite son.

The Young Men's Chorus shared the bill with the Medfield High School Concert Choir, a symbol of how much the Handel and Haydn Society had, by necessity as much as aspiration, come to share the realization of Mason's public-school mission. The solid place of music in public-school education that Mason had worked for was no longer so solid. Whereas, in the nineteenth century, Society President J. Baxter Upham could feel assured that, thanks to the rise of music education, "we shall not be at a loss for material wherewith to recruit our ranks," in the twenty-first century it was H&H itself, via education and outreach, that would increasingly be tasked with insurance against loss.

In terms of both reach and diversity, education remains a work in progress; such work is never finished. The preface to *The Boston Handel and Haydn Society Collection of Church Music* admitted as much: "Imperfection is the characteristic of every human effort," it warned, "and works of this nature especially will approach the ideal standard, only by a slow and gradual approximation." But the acceleration of educational initiative from the 1980s onward showed H&H acting on the rhetoric of its earliest apologists in a way surpassing anything seen in previous generations. It was, at long last, renewing a call first heard at the Society's centennial, embedded in Horatio Parker's specially composed, and long-forgotten, oratorio *Morven and the Grail*:

> *Children of earth, dream on*
> *Beyond your heaven, and dare*
> *Choose your own gold wherewith ye shall be crowned.*

John Finney conducting the Collaborative Youth Concert at Symphony Hall, 2012

In Their Own Words
Voices from the Karen S. and George D. Levy Education Program

I loved all your acting and you have voices like angels! I have never in my entire life heard such joyful music and wonderful songs.
Student, Columbus Elementary School, Medford

I like that we were able to see a different talent that people have. I've never seen people singing opera before in real life and it was really amazing.
Student, Dr. Martin Luther King, Jr. School, Cambridge

What I really liked about the program was that they entertained us with music and history at the same time.
Student, Stoklosa Middle School, Lowell

The more Saturday Young Women's Chorus rehearsals I have attended, the more I have fallen in love with the timeless beauty of classical music, and music in general. The music theory classes have taught me almost everything I know about that difficult part of vocal training, and I am so grateful to Handel and Haydn for offering those classes each week. On a personal level, I have met some really talented and great people through VAP. These new friends and mentors inspire me to work harder and to learn from their musical styles. The memories of going into Boston every Saturday, singing beautiful music with newfound friends, and learning while laughing in music theory class will continue to bring me joy as I move forward in my musical training and in my life.
Jessica, Young Women's Chorus

The idea of being able to apply your voice amongst the lyrics of Bach and Mozart in conjunction with many others and an orchestra is out of this world. I believe one cannot truly appreciate classical music until they are fully exposed to it. It is safe to say that the Handel and Haydn outreach program has allowed myself and many other students to appreciate classical music. It is a wonderful feeling when you work on something vigorously in a classroom and then have the ability to perform with fellow classmates, a live orchestra, and all under the wonderful John Finney. Seeing and hearing the orchestra with the wonderful soloists make me even more grateful for this opportunity because they symbolize what hard work and dedication leads to.
Cheyenne, Brockton High School
Collaborative Youth Concert participant

The most challenging and fulfilling collaborative effort my chorus makes each year is in conjunction with the Handel and Haydn Society. Every year we perform a major choral work with H&H as part of their Collaborative Youth Concerts. The piece is often in Latin and very long. Initially, the students don't believe that they will ever perform it successfully but they go along with me as I push, prod, and encourage them through our rehearsals. In the end, to their surprise but not mine, they perform the piece with pride and confidence. The highlight of my year is watching their faces light up as they sing with the orchestra or stand next to one of the soloists. In the process of learning and performing this wonderful music, they have come to love classical music, improve their ability to read notes, and take pride in their accomplishment.

The students in my chorus vary widely in their approach to learning. Some students are diligent, disciplined, and confident while others harbor a great deal of self-doubt and often give up easily when faced with a project that appears to be too demanding. The students learn so much more than just the music when they master a major choral work.

One of the benefits of a chorus—by nature a group effort—is that the students who would rather give up are carried along by the momentum and efforts of the entire ensemble. If they can actually sing forty pages of difficult music in Latin, they begin to think that they may be able to accomplish things in their other classes that they felt they couldn't do. Instead of giving up when they are challenged, they can approach a project in small steps, as we do in chorus, and end up figuring it out instead of feeling overwhelmed. The self-confidence that they develop in chorus carries over to all the other areas in their life.

Penny Knight, Brockton High School Choral Director

I like singing in Young Men's Chorus because songs allow me to express things that simple words never could, both to others and to myself. It's often said that music is the universal language of the world, but I think it's more than that. I think it's truly one of the only ways that you can express to yourself what you feel as well.

Emory, Young Men's Chorus

From a scale of 1–10, 10! I wish I could get your autographs! You guys are beautiful singers! I also want your CD if you have one!

Student, Tobin K–8 School, Cambridge

TERESA M. NEFF

THE SOCIETY AND ITS MEMBERS

JAMES SHARP joined H&H on October 15, 1816. He was a chorus member and soloist, served on the Board of Trustees three times, and served as vice president of the Society from 1828 to 1829. During a meeting to honor Benjamin B. Davis's 50th year as an H&H member, Sharp recalled how he became a member:

In 1816 I had passed twenty years of my early life in England,—that twenty years which usually determines and fixes a man's tastes and habits. Music, vocal music was my passion, and I had lived in a community that encouraged it.... and when, on Saturday, April 3, I went on board the ship *Minerva* for Boston, I gave to my friends my little musical library, supposing, of course, that I should never again, till I returned to England, hear an anthem, much less an oratorio.... I arrived in the town of Boston, and although a stranger and a foreigner, I soon found hospitality and friendship. [I] had been in Boston perhaps two weeks, when one Sunday evening I took my solitary walk across some fields which were then called Rowes Pastures. The day was closing,... and as I passed a house where I could see the happy family gathered around the evening lamp, I felt my loneliness.... Just at this moment, while my feelings were thus subdued, a breath of soft and distant music floated in the air around me, so peculiar and so unexplained that my fancy almost suggested some supernatural energy.

Listening,... I ascertained more and more distinctly the *theme* that had so fascinated me. It was the favorite minor-keyed and well-remembered subject of one of Handel's choruses, "And He shall purify the sons of Levi." You may imagine that I, by entreaty, found admittance to the meeting. That evening I witnessed for the first time a rehearsal of the Handel and Haydn Society,—a society in whose ranks and whose engagements I have passed some of the happiest hours of fifty years of my life; and the most valuable and constant friendships I have known have been friendships commenced by acquaintance on that memorable evening.

OPPOSITE
H&H Period
Instrument
Orchestra
and Chorus
performing at
Symphony Hall,
2013

Sharp's memories of his first encounter with the Handel and Haydn Society encapsulate the very essence of what H&H is about: people who share a love for music. There are many impressive statistics surrounding the Society, but perhaps none speaks to its appeal like the growth in membership during the nineteenth century. In 1815, the chorus numbered one hundred (ninety men and ten women), accompanied by a hired orchestra of twelve (some of the orchestra were H&H members, but, unlike chorus members, the orchestra was paid); by 1865, there were seven hundred chorus members. After this peak, membership settled to an average of about three hundred for the latter half of the century.

In looking at the total number of chorus members—men who were official members and women who were not considered members but counted in the chorus—in the nineteenth century, 1,717 men sang with H&H. Between 1865—when the first records of women singers were kept consistently—and 1891, 2,352 women sang with the Society as invited guests. The numbers reverse somewhat with the beginning of the twentieth century: 1,342 women and 2,280 men sang in the chorus between 1891 and 1933.

In the first half of the twentieth century, the size of the chorus averaged about two hundred. Later a new definition of "member," broadened to include the ever-growing group of supporters, most of whom did not perform, emerged with the professionalization of the chorus, approved in March 1980, and the establishment of an H&H orchestra.

James Sharp's recollections also speak to the sense of community engendered by the Society from its beginning. This, of course, assumes a common musical heritage, specifically the music of Handel, and Sharp shared a love of this music—indeed, on his first chance encounter he recognized the piece being rehearsed. This aspect of a musical society that transcends other factors (political, economic, gender, social) has always been part of H&H and contributes to long associations with the Society, some even spanning multiple generations.

Sharp was a member of H&H for some five decades. That kind of longevity is not uncommon throughout the Society's history. One of the founding members, Matthew S. Parker, was secretary from 1815 to 1819, after which he served on the Board of Trustees until 1831. He was elected to the Board twice more, and was treasurer from 1840 until his death in 1866. A member for as long as there was a Society, Parker served on the Board for almost forty-eight years.

More recently, Board member Howard Fuguet came to his first *Messiah* performance in December 1956; he returned the next year with his (future) wife, Darcy. H&H continues to be a part of their family tradition. Another Board member,

Christopher Yens, whose parents also served on the H&H Board, began coming to *Messiah* performances with his parents when he was seven years old.

Long-standing tenure with H&H was common enough that the by-laws adopted in 1890 included a provision to acknowledge members who retired after more than twenty years of successive service. Each received an "honorary ticket instead of an active chorus ticket" to be used for admission to all public performances and rehearsals.

Chorus members Mrs. Irene (Eberhard) Weitz, soprano, and Miss Doris Kennedy, alto, were given their retired members' tickets in 1950. Both had joined H&H in 1927, and sang with the chorus for twenty-three years. On June 8, 1950, Albert E. Keleher, bass, was given a standing ovation at the annual meeting for his fifty-year membership with H&H. Mrs. Grace Estes retired from the Society in 1937. She had sung for fifty years; for twenty-seven of those years, she had missed only one rehearsal, due to the death of her husband.

PRAISES LONG RECORD OF MRS GRACE ESTES

Pres Guild Reelected by Handel and Haydn Society

The attendance record of Mrs Grace G. Estes at the rehearsals and concerts of the Handel and Haydn Society was

MRS GRACE F. ESTES

praised by Pres Courtenay Guild of the society at the annual meeting at 491 Boylston st, Boston, last night. Mr Guild said that Mrs Estes had been a member of the chorus of the society 46 years and had not been absent or tardy from a rehearsal or concert during the past 23 years.

Mrs Estes, who lives at 87 School st, Roxbury, is a member of the contralto section. She sang in the concert given last April 23.

Mr Guild was reelected president for his 18th year. John C. Broadbent was elected vice president, George M. Brooks treasurer, George Banks librarian, and George F. Hatch secretary. Members of the board of governors were also elected.

Business reports for the year were given.

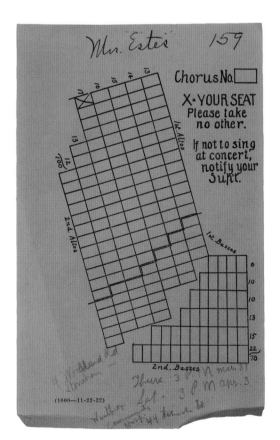

1932 seating plan showing Mrs. Grace Estes' seat in the chorus. She sang with H&H for fifty years, from 1887 to 1937. *Boston Daily Globe*, May 9, 1933

Dr. George Geyer, H&H president 1962–1974 and 1981–1983, and Jerome Preston, Jr., H&H president 1983–1986, received the H&H Medal in 1990 for their contributions to the Society

George Geyer was one of the longest-tenured H&H governors in the twentieth century. He became a chorus member in 1945; for forty years he sang in the chorus and as soloist, including the 1977 recording of *Messiah* conducted by Thomas Dunn. He served as H&H president for two terms and was one of the guiding forces as the Society transitioned from an all-volunteer chorus to a professional one. A pediatrician, Dr. Geyer was equally well-known as a medical consultant for singers.

In 1996, Geyer wrote an article for the H&H magazine *Overture* in which he explains the change in what being a member of the Society means: "Technically speaking, the members of the chorus [now professional] are not members of the Society, which is comprised of the Board of Governors and Board of Overseers. In the minds of some, however, the Chorus *is* the Society." Geyer explains that, historically, H&H members sang in the chorus, but that H&H is now a "professional chorus and an independent governing body elected from the community-at-large."

From its very beginnings, the Handel and Haydn Society established itself as a serious organization. On February 9, 1816, that is, within two months of its first public performance, the Society was "made a body politic and Corporation for the purpose of extending the knowledge and improving the style of performance of Church music."

"Old Hundred" from *The Handel and Haydn Society Collection of Church Music*. Two hundred H&H members led the singing of this hymn from the balcony of the Massachusetts State House on New Year's Eve, 1899

Potential members to the Society could be admitted only by unanimous vote. The penalty for an unexcused absence was a 50¢ fine, somewhat steep for 1815. There were four offices—president, vice president, secretary, and treasurer—in addition to eight members elected to the Board of Trustees, renamed the Board of Directors in 1867. A candidate needed seven-eighths of the members present to be elected to an office. In March 1816, the position of librarian and purveyor was added.

Responsibilities were divided among the officers. The president conducted rehearsals and performances, assigned members to a voice part, and chose the music to be sung at regular meetings. The secretary recorded the minutes of all meetings, including music sung, and maintained all correspondence. In the early years, this meant contracts for any soloists. The secretary also recorded receipts from concerts and turned the money over to the treasurer. The treasurer paid bills; expenditures also required the endorsement of the president. The librarian and purveyor secured music and refreshments—usually "spirits"—for all meetings.

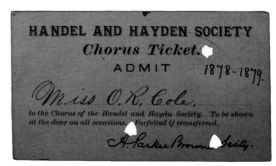

Chorus tickets were issued to members and used as a way of keeping track of individual members' attendance at meetings and performances. Member meetings were devoted to singing (rehearsals) and Board meetings conducted the business of the Society, although even these often concluded with singing.

In 1890, new by-laws reflected the realities of the Society as it then existed. The Board was charged with choosing the program for the season, judging the qualification of potential new members, and managing "everything which the interest of the Society may in their judgment demand."

Members needed to be approved by three-quarters of the Board present, sign the by-laws, and pay a $5.00 fee; however, women paid "no admission fee or assessment being simply members of the chorus and not of the corporation." If a member was found guilty of misconduct, two-thirds of the members present at a business meeting could "expel the offender." Also, if a member left his seat at any public performance or rehearsal, or if a member missed two consecutive regular rehearsals without an excuse, his membership was forfeited.

There were two different types of meetings. If one was devoted to music, i.e., a rehearsal, "no debate or discussion of any question shall be allowed." In general, there were no rehearsals from May through September. Throughout the rest of the year, there were weekly meetings for the "practice of music." Meetings could be called by the president, a majority of the Board (who could also cancel or add meetings), or by

James Williams

Thomas W. Campbell

Miss Bella Paine

Miss A. E. Brigham

BY-LAWS

OF THE

Handel and Haydn Society.

OPPOSITE
Cover of the
H&H by-laws

twenty or more members, who had to make their request in writing. Although the Society had hired a separate conductor since 1847, there was still an option for the president to conduct, or "a suitable musical director may be appointed at the discretion of the Board."

Although the only requirement for membership in the early years of the Society was a good singing voice, there is no record of members being tested. Gradually that began to change, particularly as the number of members and Ladies of the Chorus swelled and a greater variety of pieces (some more difficult) were programmed. With the 1890 by-laws, the Board had the power to suspend a member they found "incompetent to sing the music to be performed."

So the policies adopted in the 1890s remained in effect through much of the twentieth century. Voice committees were formed to test potential members; in the records for 1902–1903, the voice committee "examined for admission 323 of whom 94 were accepted." In this same account, the deaths of two members, James L. Mills and George S. Cheney, were recorded; Cheney had sung with the Society for more than thirteen years and Mills was remembered for twenty-five years of continuous service and "his constant attendance at the rehearsals and concerts."

No. ....   BOSTON, ...18

HANDEL AND HAYDN SOCIETY,
EXAMINATION FOR MEMBERSHIP.

NAME, ...

ADDRESS, ...

PROPOSED BY ....

SOP.	ALTO.	TEN.	BASS.
	Qualifications.		
READING · · ·	1.	2.	3.	4.
QUALITY · · ·	1.	2.	3.	4.
POWER · · · ·	1.	2.	3.	4.
INTONATION · · ·	1.	2.	3.	
PRONUNCIATION · ·	1.	2.	3.	
EXPRESSION · · ·	1.	2.	3.	

COMPASS,

REMARKS:

H&H audition form
used in the 1880s

The policies governing the chorus remained virtually unchanged until the 1970s, when Thomas Dunn proposed that a smaller, professional chorus be used in addition to the larger unpaid one. Chorus policy for 1977–1978 included annual membership dues of $15.00; this entitled the chorus member to be part of the corporation, the same as in 1890. Chorus membership was provisional for the first year, after which permanent membership was automatic, unless the member was notified by the Chorus Council or music director. (The last item of this policy was a strict warning that there was no smoking in the rehearsal room!)

The most fundamental change to membership came in 1980, when the Board unanimously adopted, "To remunerate all Society chorus members at a rate to be determined according to the recommendations of the National Endowment for the Arts."

About one year earlier, the Board voted to amend the by-laws of the Society, changing what it meant to be a member, now defined as anyone "who desires to further the purpose of the Society and who accepts the obligations and responsibilities of membership as evidenced by a financial or other contribution to its support…. Thus anyone wishing to become a Member has it in his power to do so. In contrast, to become a Corporator, a person is not required to make a contribution, but one must be elected."

The founding of H&H addressed the need for making music as a community, a group with a common interest. Such an endeavor needed not only organizational expertise but also musical guidance. In the early years the musical needs were satisfied by Gottlieb Graupner, founder, leader of the orchestra, and a professional musician who owned a music retail business, and his wife, Catherine, who was a soloist for the first concerts. Their daughter, also named Catherine, was organist at King's Chapel and accompanied the second H&H concert in January 1816, when the Society's organist, Samuel Taylor, became ill. She later married George Cushing, H&H founder and flutist in the orchestra. Gottlieb Graupner did not hold any elected office in the Society; since his retail business often secured music for the Society, he may have refrained from serving on the Board to avoid any appearance of a conflict of interest relating to rules that prohibited any H&H member from profiting from a performance of the Society. That the Society paid for the Graupners' hackney carriage to the first concert is an indication of their stature in Boston's musical world.

Another family closely associated with H&H, in fact created by it, was the Ostinellis. Sophia Hewitt, organist of the Society in the 1820s, married concertmaster Louis Ostinelli. Although the Board's appointment of another organist, Charles Zeuner, in 1830, was controversial, the Society remained supportive, singing as part

LEFT
Payment to H&H organist
Sophia Hewitt Ostinelli, 1830

BELOW
Program for February 1849 concert
featuring Eliza (Ostinelli) Biscaccianti

ROSSINI'S STABAT MATER

WILL BE PERFORMED BY THE

HANDEL AND HAYDN SOCIETY,

AT THE MELODEON,

On Sunday Evening, February 18, 1849,

ASSISTED BY

SIGNORA BISCACCIANTI,

MISS A. STONE,

SIGNOR PERELLI, and

SIGNOR AVIGNONE.

Performance to commence at half past 7 o'clock.

The audience is requested to refrain from any expression of applause.

PART FIRST.

QUARTETTE AND CHORUS.

"Stabat mater dolorosa;
Juxta crucem lacrimosa;
  Dum pendebat Filius."

"The pious mother mourned her loss;
She stood and wept beneath the cross,
  Which bore her much loved son."

AIR, TENORE.

"Cujus animam gementem,
Contristantam et dolentem,
  Pertransivit gladius.
O quam tristis et afflicta
Fuit illa benedicta
  Mater Unigeniti!
Quæ mœrebat et dolebat,
Et tremebat, cum videbat
  Nati pœnas inclyti."

"And through her deeply wounded breast,
With sorrow's heaviest weight oppressed,
  The sword of grief was run.
Then how full of deep-felt anguish,
Did that blessed mother languish,
  For him her only love!
With trembling and with sadness worn,
How deeply did that mother mourn
  His pangs, who bled above."

DUETTO.

"Quis est homo qui non fleret
Christi matrem si videret
  In tanto supplicio?
Quis non posset contristari,
Piam matrem contemplari,
  Dolentem cum Filio?"

Where is the man, who all unmoved,
Could see her, who so truly loved,
  Thus sunk in bitter grief?
The painful scene who could have borne?
So pure a soul with anguish torn,
  And none to yield relief?

AIR, BASSO.

"Pro peccatis suæ gentis,
Vidit Jesum in tormentis,
Et flagellis subditum.
Vidit suum dulcem Natum
Morientem, desolatum,
  Dum emisit spiritum."

"She saw his blood profusely shed,
For his own people's crimes he bled,
  From stripes and cruel blows;
She saw her sweet and only child,
In desolation, calm, and mild
  In life's expiring throes."

BASSO, SOLO AND CHORUS.

Eia mater fons amoris,
Me sentire vim doloris,
  Fac ut tecum lugeam.
Fac ut ardeat cor meum
In amando Christum Deum,
  Ut sibi complaceam."

"Hear then, O mother! source of love,
Let me thy bitter sorrows prove,
  And let me weep with thee.
May my poor heart be all on fire,
With Christ's bright love, let my desire,
  To please him ever be."

PART SECOND.

QUARTUOR.

"Sancta mater istud agas,
Crucifixi fige plagas
  Cordi meo valida,
Tui nati vulnerati,
Jam dignati pro me pati,
  Pœnas medum divide.
Fac me vere tecum flere'
Crucifixo condolere,
  Donec ego vixero.
Juxta crucem tecum stare,
Te libenter sociare,
  In planctu desidero.
Virgo virginum præclara,
Mihi jam non sis amara,
  Fac me tecum plangere."

"Let his wounds make deep impression,
Let them hold a sweet possession,
  Firm in my faithful heart;
Let no joys my fond love sever:
In his pains O let me ever
  Suffer with thee a part.
O make me truly weep with thee,
Mourning with him who died for me,
  Let me in grief expire;
By his loved cross, with thee to stay,
With thee to tread the painful way,
  Such is my fond desire.
Virgin, above all Virgins blest!
All my poor longing heart's request
  Is with thy grief to mourn."

CAVATINE.

"Fac ut portem christi mortem,
Passionis fac confortem,
  Et plagas recolere,
Fac me plagis vulnerari,
Cruce hac inebriari,
  Ob amorem Filii;"

"O may I bear my Saviour's death,
Treasuring until my latest breath,
  All that his love has borne.
Let me my Saviour's sufferings share,
And his sweet cross devoutly bear,
  For thy own Son's pure love."

AIR AND CHORUS.

"Inflammatus et accensus,
Per te Virgo sim defensus,
  In die judicii,
Fac me cruce custodiri
Morte Christi præmuniri,
  Confoveri gratia."

"And burning with love's holy fire,
O screen me from the vengeful ire
  Of my great judge above.
May the bright cross my guardian be,
My Saviour's death defence to me,
  And source of every grace."

QUARTUOR.

"Quando corpus morietur,
Fac ut animæ donetur
  Paradisi gloria."

"And when my body meets decay,
Obtain my soul in that dread day,
  In Paradise a place."

FINALE.

"Amen. In sempiterna sæcula,
amen."

"Amen; for ever, amen!"

Oakes & Solomons, State Street.

Piano builder Jonas Chickering and his sons all served as president of H&H

UPPER LEFT
Jonas Chickering,
H&H president 1843–1850

UPPER RIGHT
Charles Francis Chickering,
H&H president 1856–1858

LOWER LEFT
Thomas Chickering,
H&H president 1858–1861

LOWER RIGHT
George Chickering,
H&H president 1887–1888

of a benefit concert for Sophia in May 1833. The Ostinellis' daughter, Eliza, studied voice and became one of the great opera and concert singers in Europe and America; she returned to sing with H&H in 1848.

Musical families continued to influence H&H throughout the nineteenth century. The Chickerings, a famous family of Boston piano manufacturers, were members; their firm donated instruments and later the use of Chickering Hall for rehearsals and performances. Jonas Chickering (1798–1853) learned to build pianos in 1820; over the rest of the century, Chickering and Sons was one of the premier piano builders in the country, patenting the cast-iron frame that allowed for a fuller sound in both the square and grand pianos.

For seventy years, the Chickerings sang, served on the Board, and brought new musical compositions to the Society's repertoire. Jonas Chickering joined H&H in 1818. He sang tenor, both as a chorus member and soloist, and served as a trustee, vice-president, and president (1843–1850). In 1848, he returned from a trip to England with a copy of the score for Mendelssohn's *Elijah*; he urged H&H to learn the oratorio and it became a staple in the Society's repertoire.

The first H&H president, Thomas Smith Webb, sang the duet "Come, ever-smiling Liberty" from Handel's *Judas Maccabaeus* with Mrs. Withington at the first H&H concert

Like James Sharp and Jonas Chickering, soloists were often the president of the Society. Amasa Winchester, a founding member, sang in the chorus and was a frequent soloist. According to an author for the Boston music magazine *Euterpiæd*, he sang "with a fine body of voice, much true feeling, much exquisite taste, and a very distinct yet musical pronunciation." Winchester, who served as the first vice-president and then president from 1819 to 1822, and again from 1825 to 1827, was regarded for his tact and diplomatic nature as much as his musical talent. When the more abrasive Lowell Mason succeeded Winchester as president (and conductor), Mason criticized the playing of one of the trombonists, who immediately left the rehearsal. Mason reportedly asked how Winchester would have handled the situation. The reply: "He would have tapped very lightly on his desk and said that trombone is very beautiful, but we will try the piece without it and see how it sounds." Diplomacy and exacting standards did not frequently combine in one individual; Amasa Winchester gained a reputation for both.

H&H President Charles Callahan Perkins lived and traveled in Europe before
returning to Boston. A composer, he was the first American to be published by the
German firm Breitkopf & Härtel. He was one of the founders of the Massachusetts
Normal Art School (today the Massachusetts College of Art and Design, or MassArt).
He was an incorporator of the Museum of Fine Arts in Boston and advocated the
need to exhibit works of antiquity as well as contemporary art. Perkins, who served
as H&H president from 1850 to 1851, and again from 1875 until his death in 1886,
was also a major contributor to Boston Music Hall and donated a bronze statue of
Beethoven by his friend Thomas Crawford for the new performing space. On July 28,
1899, the statue was moved from Music Hall to the Boston Public Library; later, it was
moved to the Huntington Avenue foyer at the New England Conservatory, where it
stands today.

The Crawford statue was just one connection between H&H and Beethoven. The
Society performed Beethoven's music early in its history and confirmed its commitment to new music by commissioning an oratorio from the great composer.

Beethoven never fulfilled the commission, but the Society continued to perform
his works. His Symphony No. 7 was performed as part of the Society's 50th Anniversary Festival. The Society's concert on December 19, 1870, marked the culmination
of a week-long celebration for Beethoven's centennial. His Symphony No. 9 was the
featured work; the *Egmont* Overture, the quartet from *Fidelio*, the Andante and Ada-
gio from *The Creatures of Prometheus,* and the "Hallelujah" Chorus from *Christ on the
Mount of Olives* completed the program.

Statue of Beethoven by Thomas Crawford, currently in the foyer of New England Conservatory's Jordan Hall, Boston

Handel and Haydn Society

THE BEACH MASS

IN E FLAT

ORIGINAL PRODUCTION OF THE WORK

FOLLOWED BY

THE CHORAL FANTASIA OF BEETHOVEN

SUNDAY, FEBRUARY 7, 1892, AT 7.30

It adds a peculiar pleasure to our season to have the privilege of performing such a work as this by a Boston composer, heightened by the fact that the composer is a Boston lady. The announcement of the completion of the Mass has been received in the community with the keenest interest; and those who have obtained acquaintance with it are unanimous in their admiration of its beauty, brilliancy, and strength. A work of such magnitude by a woman makes a positive addition to the history of music; and its approaching production will not only be an event of capital importance in the musical life of the city, but will have a far more than local interest and significance.

The quartet of solo singers will be recognized as appropriate to the brilliant work and commensurate with the importance of the occasion. Mrs. Beach will crown the eventful evening by playing the piano part in the Choral Fantasia.

MRS. JENNIE PATRICK WALKER, Soprano
MRS. CARL ALVES, Alto
MR. ITALO CAMPANINI, Tenor
MR. EMIL FISCHER, Bass

Mrs. H. H. A. BEACH, Pianist

MR. CARL ZERRAHN, Conductor
MR. B. J. LANG, Organist

Tickets for sale at Music Hall on and after Monday, February 1;
$2, $1.50, and $1, according to location.

CHARLES W. STONE,
Secretary.

On January 1, 1863, members of the Society, including Julia Ward Howe, author of the *Battle Hymn of the Republic*, performed portions of Mendelssohn's *Hymn of Praise* and *Elijah* plus the "Hallelujah" Chorus from *Messiah* at the celebration surrounding the reading of the Emancipation Proclamation in Boston. Ralph Waldo Emerson read his poem *Boston Hymn* as part of a "Grand Jubilee Concert" in Boston Music Hall.

On February 7, 1892, Beethoven's Choral Fantasy was paired with the premiere of Amy Beach's Mass in E-flat, Op. 5, the first work by a female composer performed by the Society. An accomplished pianist, Beach was also the soloist for the Beethoven on the concert. Newspaper coverage of this concert ranged from descriptions of the large audience to a glowing review ("She has fixed ideas of her own and she has not hesitated to carry them out"), to an article by former H&H chorus member Julia Ward Howe, who wrote that the Mass "gave great pleasure to the lovers of good music" with its "unmistakable fervor and feeling."

One twentieth-century H&H president, Courtenay Guild, was related to a founder of the Society, Jacob Guild. Guild was president from 1915 to 1946; he guided the Society during two world wars and an intervening economic depression. During his tenure, H&H refocused its organizational component by hiring a business manager to help with duties normally assigned to officers and to increase ticket sales. In this way, the business side of the Society was part of a new organizational model that recognized managing the financial side of the Society and making music required different skills. The remainder of the twentieth century would be a redefining of both music and organization for the Society; however, what never got lost was the sense of community. It was, in fact, celebrated and encouraged. The parameters of the music and business might change, but the dedication to the ideal of music, while interpreted differently, was never questioned.

GEORGE FREDERICK HANDEL'S

"Messiah"

PRESENTED BY THE

| SYMPHONY HALL | HANDEL and HAYDN SOCIETY | SUN. EVE. 8:15 DEC. 19 |

| RUTH DIEHL
Soprano
WESLEY COPPLESTONE
Tenor | DR. THOMPSON STONE
CONDUCTOR | SONIA ESSIN
Contralto
WALTER KIDDER
Bass |

55 MEMBERS OF THE
BOSTON SYMPHONY ORCHESTRA

1742=1943

Two Hundred One Years Since Its First Performance

TODAY
...NO OTHER MUSICAL COMPOSITION
IS HELD IN SUCH UNIVERSAL
AFFECTION AS IS HANDEL'S

"Messiah"

The Story of Christmas Magnificently Told in Music

THIS MONUMENTAL WORK CAN
MOVE OUR SOULS—ITS CONCEPTION
IS ONE OF THE SUBLIMEST THAT
COULD ENGAGE THE ATTENTION
OF THE HUMAN MIND.

The first manager (or business agent, as the position was named in 1928) for the Society was Anita Davis-Chase. From this point forward, H&H would supplement the work of the Board with an office staff. In the second half of the twentieth century, as the Society placed new emphasis on performances, education, and fundraising, building an administrative staff became vital.

In the 1980s, the Society sought a new direction musically and administratively. The professionalization of the chorus was the first step in what would be a transformation of H&H from an amateur ensemble with membership limited to chorus members to an ensemble of professional singers and instrumentalists dedicated to performance techniques more closely related to those of the late seventeenth and eighteenth centuries. When Christopher Hogwood came to H&H in 1986, he created a period-instrument ensemble within the larger orchestra, much as Thomas Dunn had established a smaller professional chorus within the larger one. Hogwood asked Daniel Stepner to be concertmaster for both the modern and period-instrument orchestras. During his twenty-four years leading the orchestra, Stepner also conducted and soloed with the Society.

Daniel Stepner, violin, and Stephen Hammer, oboe, performing with the H&H Period Instrument Orchestra at Jordan Hall, 2008

OPPOSITE
Announcement for *Messiah* performance, December 1943

All sections of the orchestra now had players who specialized in historically informed performance. Stephen Hammer, principal oboe and recorder; Christopher Krueger, principal flute; and Eric Hoepner, principal clarinet, formed the core of the woodwind section under Christopher Hogwood. They continue in these roles today, along with Andrew Schwartz, principal bassoon, who came to the orchestra in 1987.

Timpanist John Grimes began playing for H&H under Thomas Dunn. Like many musicians during this time, Grimes played on both modern and historical instruments. He played with H&H for more than thirty years, under five music directors, until his untimely death in the summer of 2013.

James David Christie, continuo player, acted as an advisor to Hogwood as he retooled the H&H orchestra. Christie also suggested the virtuoso keyboardist, John Finney, as chorus master in 1990. Named associate conductor in 1992, Finney's role with H&H continually expanded as he programmed and conducted regular season performances, such as the annual Christmas concert, and became the much-loved leader of the Collaborative Youth Concerts.

At the turn of the twenty-first century, the Society experienced an artistic renaissance and presented a series of innovative programs combining semi-staged operas, dance, and visually stunning productions along with touring and recording schedules. Undertaking this kind of fundamental reorientation of the Society could not be achieved only in performance; there needed to be strong organizational and administrative support to complement the vision of the Board which encouraged, and even engineered, a new direction for H&H, enlarging its definition of membership while redefining its role in terms of performance. Under H&H President Jerome (Jerry) Preston, Mary (Hall) Deissler was named general manager, a position that allowed her to work more closely with the Board. The long-term and concerted efforts of H&H Presidents Mitchell Adams, J. Anthony Lloyd, Robert Scott, and Janet Whitla, along with the managerial skills of Deissler, altered the course of the Society. With some initial financial assistance from the National Arts Stabilization Fund, from the 1980s through the turn of the twenty-first century, the Society gradually expanded the number of concerts in its season and went from running a deficit to operating with a surplus.

The Board today is no longer concerned with choosing repertoire and adjudicating singers; rather, it is a group that provides oversight and stewardship to all facets of the Society. Board members, from a variety of backgrounds and professions, contribute the individual expertise drawn from their diverse experiences to give the Society strategic direction. For example, the Education Committee of the H&H Board spearheaded a program for school-age children designed to bring music into the

Fay Chandler, H&H patron, Mary Deissler, H&H Executive Director 1985–2007,
and Richard Ortner, H&H Board of Overseers, 1999–2010

Dean and Janet Whitla, first female president
of H&H, 2000–2005

Robert H. Scott, H&H president 1992–2000,
Mitchell Adams, H&H president 1986–1900,
and Christopher Hogwood

Joseph Flynn, H&H treasurer
1986–2012

George and Karen Levy, H&H Board of Governors

classroom and give young singers the opportunity to perform together and occasionally with the professional ensemble.

Marie-Hélène Bernard was appointed executive director and chief executive officer of the Society in April 2007. Her legal and musical background combined with her arts administration experience with major U.S. orchestras allowed her to guide the Society and its Board with a sure hand as the organization prepared for its Bicentennial. After stabilizing the finances and restructuring the organization, the Board and Bernard crafted a strategic plan and commissioned a campaign feasibility study that led to the adoption of ambitious artistic, educational, and community initiatives and impressive Bicentennial plans. Under Bernard's leadership, H&H received multiple gifts of one million dollars each, the largest donations in its history: in 2012, the chorus was funded in perpetuity by Jane and Wat Tyler and the Education Program was funded in perpetuity by Karen S. and George D. Levy. A third one-million-dollar gift was made in 2013, a tremendous achievement for an organization that operates on a $3.5 million annual budget. With a growing endowment, H&H officially opened its Bicentennial celebrations with the 2014–2015 Season.

H&H has redefined itself and what it means to be a member of the Society over the course of its history. For more than one hundred and fifty years, only male singers

Marie-Hélène Bernard, H&H Executive Director & CEO 2007–present, Wat Tyler, H&H Board of Governors, Jane Tyler, and Harry Christophers

in the chorus were counted as members. From this group, the Board and officers were chosen and the organization managed through them. Women always sang with the Society, even if they were not always acknowledged as members. The first changes to the Society occurred in relation to musical standards; conductors were hired, repertoire became more challenging, and members were tested. In the twentieth century, business managers were added to help meet the growing organizational needs of the Society. Yet even as the Society looked beyond its members for business managers, it looked within its ranks for its conductors, first Thompson Stone and then Edward Gilday, before taking a new direction. During Thomas Dunn's tenure, the chorus was made professional and, technically speaking, no longer members of the Society. With that, H&H amended its definition of member, broadening it to include anyone who shares the same passion for music, just as James Sharp recognized almost two hundred years ago. In 2014, that includes a chorus of forty-four, an orchestra of seventy-one, a professional staff of twenty-four, twenty-two volunteers, thirty governors, thirty-five overseers, some 2,600 subscribers, and thousands more individual ticket buyers, plus the Vocal Arts Program of 143 singers and the Education Program that reaches 10,000 students each year. Like James Sharp, these members, too, will have passed "some of the happiest hours" as members of the Society.

PAGES 144–145
H&H scrapbook pages showing sample tickets for concerts in 1901, 1904, and 1905

Handel and Haydn Society

December 25, 1904 · February 19, 1905 · April 23, 1905 · December 26, 1904 — FLOOR

$2.00 — 1 1 · $2.50 — 3 3 · $2.00 — V E 1 4 · $2.00 — 2 2

Handel and Haydn Society — Ninetieth Season
MESSIAH
BOSTON SYMPHONY HALL
Sunday, December 25, 1904, at 7.30 P. M.
$2.00
William H. Bradbury, Secretary.

Handel and Haydn Society — Ninetieth Season
MISCELLANEOUS CONCERT
Soloist, Mme. Nordica
BOSTON SYMPHONY HALL
Sunday, February 19, 1905, at 7.30 P. M.
$2.50
William H. Bradbury, Secretary.

Handel and Haydn Society — Ninetieth Season
CREATION
BOSTON SYMPHONY HALL
Easter Sunday, April 23, 1905, at 7.30 P. M.
$2.00
William H. Bradbury, Secretary.

Handel and Haydn Society — Ninetieth Season
MESSIAH
BOSTON SYMPHONY HALL
Monday, December 26, 1904, at 7.30 P. M.
$2.00
William H. Bradbury, Secretary.

Handel and Haydn Society

December 25, 1904 · February 19, 1905 · April 23, 1905 · December 26, 1904 — FLOOR

$1.50 — $27.50 — 1 1 · $1.50 — X 31 3 · $1.50 — X 31 4 · $1.50 — X 31 2

Handel and Haydn Society — Ninetieth Season
MESSIAH
BOSTON SYMPHONY HALL
Sunday, December 25, 1904, at 7.30 P. M.
$1.50
William H. Bradbury, Secretary.

Handel and Haydn Society — Ninetieth Season
MISCELLANEOUS CONCERT
Soloist, Mme. Nordica
BOSTON SYMPHONY HALL
Sunday, February 19, 1905, at 7.30 P. M.
$2.00
William H. Bradbury, Secretary.

Handel and Haydn Society — Ninetieth Season
CREATION
BOSTON SYMPHONY HALL
Easter Sunday, April 23, 1905, at 7.30 P. M.
$1.50
William H. Bradbury, Secretary.

Handel and Haydn Society — Ninetieth Season
MESSIAH
BOSTON SYMPHONY HALL
Monday, December 26, 1904, at 7.30 P. M.
$1.50
William H. Bradbury, Secretary.

Handel and Haydn Society

December 25, 1904 · February 19, 1905 · April 23, 1905 · December 26, 1904 — SECOND BALCONY CENTRE

$1.00 — 1 1 · $1.50 — 3 3 · $1.00 — 4 4 · $1.00 — D 28 2 2

HANDEL AND HAYDN SOCIETY

MR. EMIL MOLLENHAUER, CONDUCTOR

MR. H. G. TUCKER, ORGANIST

LAST CONCERT OF HANDEL AND HAYDN IN MUSIC HALL

ELIJAH

SUNDAY, APRIL 15, 1900, AT 7.30 P.M.

MME. GADSKI, Soprano
Miss MARIAN VAN DUYN, Contralto
MR. CLARENCE B. SHIRLEY, Tenor
MR. GWILYM MILES, Bass

¶ TICKETS ON SALE AT MUSIC HALL DURING THE WEEK BEGINNING APRIL 9. $2, $1.50, $1

WILLIAM F. BRADBURY, SECRETARY
NUMBER 369 HARVARD STREET, CAMBRIDGE

STEVEN LEDBETTER

A NEW CENTURY: 1900–1967

IT IS RARE for a musical organization to be led by the same conductor for four decades or more. Such longstanding activity, especially in an organization made up mostly of amateur musicians, naturally generates warm feelings on the part of the members, feelings of gratitude for long years of devoted service, and also concerns that age may be diminishing the quality of the leader's work.

Carl Zerrahn had achieved a prodigious amount in building the musical quality of the Handel and Haydn Society chorus, at least during parts of his long tenure. Having begun his service at the age of twenty-six as a flutist, who had arrived in Boston with the Germania Orchestra in 1848, he turned his skill and energy to building the quality of the ensemble and enlarging its repertory. He also conducted choral organizations in Salem and Worcester for several decades. But after four decades with H&H, he was apparently losing steam, a fact that might have been hinted subtly to him. In any case, in 1894 he volunteered to retire, setting off several years of argument and crisis.

There was a strong movement to replace Zerrahn with B.J. Lang, who had been organist of the Society's concerts since 1859. Lang had many other strings to his bow. He was a composer, a busy teacher of organ and piano (his most significant pupil was the composer Arthur Foote), a creator of choruses—the all-male Apollo Club and the mixed Cecilia, which still exists. With his choruses, Lang was far more advanced in his choice of repertory than the Handel and Haydn Society had ever been (for some this may have been a mark against him), and he was an important exponent of Wagner, having been one of the leaders in American fundraising for the Bayreuth Festival. For two years Lang did take over the concerts, but then a long, hot summer of strife between partisans of Lang and of Zerrahn led to the return of Zerrahn for the 1897–1898 season.

OPPOSITE
Announcement for
final H&H concert in
Boston Music Hall,
April 1900

147

Zerrahn officially retired, with full honors, after conducting Mendelssohn's *Elijah* on May 2, 1898, closing a career with the Society lasting some forty-four years. His retirement resolved what the Society's historian for 1897–1898 regarded as the most severe crisis in its history. But matters were not yet settled.

Boston had a number of fine native-born musicians who might well have taken over the reins. Most notable among these was the composer George Whitefield Chadwick, an energetic man in his mid-forties. He had a long personal history with the Society, in youth eagerly attending the Triennial Festival concerts in 1871 and 1874. He missed the 1877 festival, but by 1880 he was on the program as a composer, having just returned from studies in Leipzig and Munich to conduct his first orchestral work, the overture *Rip Van Winkle*. On February 5, 1893, the Society performed his cantata *Phoenix expirans*. In 1897, Chadwick leaped into the breach when Lang was down with pneumonia, conducting *Messiah* without a rehearsal, and thereby missing the first performance of his String Quartet No. 4, which the Kneisel Quartet was premiering that night.

Chadwick might reasonably have expected to be invited to conduct the Society, especially since he had shown his ability as a choral conductor at festivals in both Springfield and Worcester. He mentioned this possibility with some acerbity in his memoirs: "The H&H folks were vociferous in my praise, both as conductor and composer, but they forgot it all a year or two later, when they needed a new conductor and sent to New York for a German singing teacher that nobody had ever heard of. And this too after I had jumped into an emergency and conducted the 'Messiah' for them without a rehearsal, when Mr Lang was ill with pneumonia."

H&H performed *Phoenix expirans*, a cantata by American composer George Whitefield Chadwick, in February 1893

Reinhold Herman,
H&H conductor
1898–1899

The "German singing teacher" to whom Chadwick referred was one Reinhold Herman, a composer of light songs and conductor of a German men's singing club (such groups were known in every city with a substantial German immigrant population). Presumably the choice was made—as happened so often in those years—because boards of musical organizations could not imagine a better choice for music director than a *German* musician, whatever his qualifications. Certainly no mere American could hope to stand at the same rank! In any case, Herman resigned after one year and returned permanently to Germany. Of course, the same candidate for music director still existed, but once again Chadwick was passed over, possibly because his new position as director of the New England Conservatory might have generated concern that he would be too busy to give his full attention to the Society.

Instead, the Board chose an American who was as close as they could get to a German conductor. Emil Mollenhauer, the son of German immigrants, was born in Brooklyn. He showed a prodigious musical talent as violinist and pianist; at the age of eight he had appeared in public as violinist at a popular entertainment location, Niblo's Theater in New York. He had early experience in theater orchestras, and later

played in some of the country's most important ensembles, the Theodore Thomas Orchestra in New York and, in the mid-1880s, the Boston Symphony Orchestra. After that he accepted the directorship of the Boston Festival Orchestra, an ensemble that accompanied local choral groups in music festivals all over the country, normally from the spring to the fall. Thus, Mollenhauer was intimately familiar with a wide range of choral masterpieces and seemed an ideal choice as a replacement for Carl Zerrahn. Indeed, he seems to have been a perfect fit, remaining active with the Society until June 1, 1927, just six months before his death.

Members were notified on September 18, 1899, by way of a printed card from the Society's secretary, William F. Bradbury, that, "Mr. Reinhold L. Herman, who was elected conductor in June, declined to accept and on September 1 the Board of Government elected Mr. Emil Mollenhauer." The new director, who was to shape the fortunes of the Society for just over a quarter century, met the singers at his first rehearsal on October 1. Soon afterward, a similar card carried a request that members seek to encourage singers of their acquaintance to audition so as to augment the size of the chorus by two hundred members (the existing membership was given as two hundred and fifty voices, but with a deficit in the tenor and bass parts, for which more singers were earnestly entreated).

On some public occasions during the Mollenhauer era, the Handel and Haydn Society chorus was invited to offer a musical selection as a participant in a civic event. On Thursday, October 12, 1899, members were notified that Boston's Mayor Quincy had invited the chorus to take part in a special presentation of a watch to Admiral Dewey, hero of the Spanish-American War. There was not much advance notice for the event, which took place only two days later.

From the very first *Messiah* performance under Mollenhauer's directorship, the press showed renewed enthusiasm for the musical results. *The Boston Journal* called it "the finest, most musical, most impressive choral and orchestral performances given by the Handel and Haydn Society during the last ten years." The choral performance, opined *The Boston Traveller*, went far beyond good. "[T]he venerable oratorio became a living, breathing, even thrilling thing again, to be enjoyed as in the days when it was a new experience."

After the conductor and musicians themselves, nothing affects the sound of a musical performance as much as the hall in which it takes place. At the turn of the century, Boston experienced its most significant development in concert venues with the opening of Symphony Hall. It was one of several buildings erected by Boston's

Rehearsal in Potter Hall, New Century Building, 177 Huntington Avenue, Boston, 1903

TOP: Symphony Hall exterior. An artist's rendering (left) before it was built. It is far more decoratively ornamented than the final red-brick version (right), which is without statues in the niches, carved swags—the structure reduced to bare-bones simplicity.
BOTTOM: Symphony Hall interior

cultural institutions that were feeling squeezed in the rapidly growing downtown area, so they were moving west along Huntington Avenue to sites with more space. Among these institutions were the Museum of Fine Arts, the New England Conservatory, the Massachusetts Horticultural Society, and the Boston Symphony Orchestra, which, since its founding, had maintained a collegial relationship with the Handel and Haydn Society.

The Boston Symphony and the Handel and Haydn Society had both performed for many years in the Boston Music Hall, but when an urban renewal project threatened to demolish the building, the time clearly came to make new plans. Henry Lee Higginson, the creator and, for all practical purposes, owner of the Boston Symphony, undertook to order the construction of a first-rate new concert hall. It was designed with the best possible attention to clear sound, as conceived by Wallace Clement Sabine, a professor at Harvard University. He created the first concert hall in the world with scientifically designed acoustics.

The new building was also to be called the Boston Music Hall. A lingering echo of that intention can be found in the iron balusters of the stairways in the new building, which contain the letters "BMH" intertwined in floral decorations. But since the original building was still standing when the new hall was ready, the name was changed to Symphony Hall. It has long been recognized as one of the world's most excellent music venues.

Just as both musical organizations had shared the Boston Music Hall for their performances, Higginson invited the Handel and Haydn Society to perform in the superb new Symphony Hall. The Boston Symphony traditionally performed on Friday afternoons and Saturday evenings. The Handel and Haydn Society had traditionally performed on Sundays, so there was no difficulty in sharing the performance space.

The dedication of Symphony Hall took place on October 15, 1900, with the regular Boston Symphony concerts beginning on the following Friday and Saturday, October 19 and 20. The very next day was the Society's first concert of the year,

Between 1902–1903, the H&H Library was located on the first balcony level of Symphony Hall

A distinguished contralto, Ernestine Schumann-Heink was a soloist with H&H for the Verdi Requiem in January 1901

"to dedicate the hall to Oratorio" with a performance of *Elijah*. The response of press and public was little short of ecstatic, both for the quality of the performance under Mollenhauer and the clarity of sound achieved in the new concert venue.

The 1900–1901 season was especially marked by a memorial performance of the Verdi Requiem less than a month after the composer's death, on January 27, 1901. The Society had performed it five times previously, but on this occasion no exertion was spared to make it a particularly memorable occasion, with a chorus of some three hundred and fifty singers, an orchestra of sixty-seven Boston Symphony members, and a fine cast of soloists, including the great contralto Ernestine Schumann-Heink.

The following year, the concerns of the Society's directors turned to the hoped-for construction of a building just for the organization, one that would combine "a hall suitable for rehearsals, facilities for a large musical library, a reading room, committee rooms, and rooms which our members can use for the study and practice of music." The rehearsal space would not only make scheduling easier, it would also provide a facility that could be rented out to some of the many choruses springing up in and around Boston. Symphony Hall was the performance venue, but it was rarely available for rehearsal since the Boston Symphony both rehearsed and performed there, and the management also rented out the hall for lectures, recitals, and even, in the early years, commercial events.

OPPOSITE
The Commemorative Record, a short history of H&H, was given to patrons at the March 8, 1903 concert

In the hope of augmenting a building fund that had been kept separate from other budgetary requirements, the season's schedule included two additional concerts especially for its benefit. These were to be the Verdi Requiem and *Elijah*, rather

The
Handel & Haydn
Society
of Boston
Commemorative Record
1815 — 1903

E·S·FISHER, Des.

daringly on two consecutive days, November 10 and 11, with a strong group of soloists who apparently donated their services. Other efforts went on for a number of years, but eventually the building fund was amalgamated into the general funds of the organization and the search for a building designed, constructed, and owned by the Handel and Haydn Society was abandoned.

Despite new and recent items included in the programs, it remained upsetting to some people that year after year the programs of the Society offered the same works, great masterpieces though they might be: *Messiah*, of course, and *The Creation*; *Elijah*; the Verdi Requiem; less often, *Judas Maccabaeus*; *St. Matthew Passion*; the Mozart Requiem; later, Elgar's *The Dream of Gerontius*; and also works that barely survived the end of the nineteenth century, including Gounod's *Redemption* and Bruch's *Arminius*. For an organization performing an average of three concerts per year for a century, that is a limited repertory indeed, and there were those who felt it was time to enlarge it.

But then, many of the singers had been members for years, if not decades, and they felt entirely at home with pieces they had sung a dozen times, while newer works threatened to make demands on their musicianship that some might not be willing or able to meet. President Bradbury died nineteen days short of his fiftieth anniversary as a member of the Society, and he came that close to singing in both the 50th and 100th anniversary concerts. A report by the organization's vice president on the occasion of the centennial explicitly celebrated the fact that they avoided modern scores, indicating that the Society was devoted only to familiar music of the past.

Ticket for Old-Home Week concert, Symphony Hall, July 1907

Program for Dubois' *Paradise Lost*,
February 1903

Mollenhauer made an effort to update and vary the repertory with mixed results, both in performance quality (the singers were not entirely comfortable with recent musical styles) and in musical value. But his effort was a worthy one, to increase the range of the Society and to make its annual offerings less predictable. Ironically, predictability often seemed to be what many ticket buyers wanted, and the Society's Board worried that novelty might reduce the size of the house for performances of anything other than the old favorites.

Among the new works was a substantial treatment of Milton's *Paradise Lost* by the French composer Théodore Dubois (1837–1924). Dubois composed the work in 1878; it received the City of Paris Prize that year following two performances in the Colonne Concerts. The Society's performance in February 1903 was the first in the United States. Dubois's choral writing was easy enough for an amateur chorus to learn, and it made a satisfyingly rich effect, but it was never again performed in these concerts. When the Society undertook another *Paradise Lost*, in 1910, it was a version by the less well-known Marco Enrico Bossi (1861–1925), who styled his work a "symphonic-vocal poem."

Six weeks before the Bossi performance, the Society had performed Arthur Sullivan's *The Golden Legend,* a dramatic cantata based on a poem by Henry Wadsworth Longfellow, which no doubt seemed especially suitable for a Boston performance. But in the quarter century since Sullivan wrote the piece, its star had faded drastically. With rare exceptions it seemed churchy in the worst Victorian sense, and lacked the life of Sullivan's Savoy operas, except when this risked getting laughter from the audience, such as the presumably dramatic moment when the heroine, Elsie, declares her willingness to give her life for the man she loves ("I come here not to argue, but to die!"), and the chorus responds with a passage that could come straight out of *H. M. S. Pinafore* ("She comes here not to argue, but to die!"). The reviews were distinctly negative, though the work was repeated in 1921.

Chadwick, whose *Phoenix expirans* had been favorably received in 1893, proposed a double bill of that short work with his more recent and longer Christmas cantata, *Noel,* in early 1911, even offering the promise of a donor who would pay for five hundred copies of the vocal score if the work were chosen—but all that happened was a repetition of *Phoenix expirans* on a mixed program in 1913.

The grandest gesture toward expanding the repertory came in connection with the Society's centennial in 1915. It was a commission for a major new work, offered to one of America's leading composers of the day, who had already shown his mettle in composing an oratorio given countless performances in the United States and England. Horatio Parker's *Hora novissima* (1893) was hailed immediately as a work of special importance. The Society had taken it up for a concert in February 1894, only

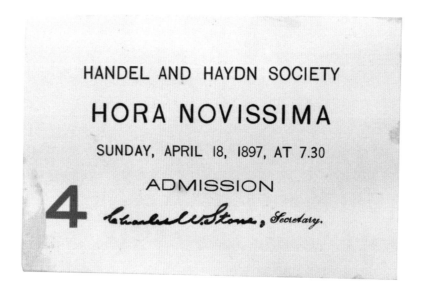

Chorus ticket for Parker's *Hora novissima*

months after the work's premiere in New York. In the meantime, Parker had won a competition that led to his *Mona* being the first American opera presented at The Metropolitan Opera.

In planning for the centennial year, the Board hoped lightning would strike again. Parker proposed to create a dramatic oratorio based on an Arthurian legend, with a text to be written by his regular collaborator, Brian Hooker, best known as the translator of Rostand's *Cyrano de Bergerac*. The new work, *Morven and the Grail*, grew over the course of the year before the festival, with increasingly urgent correspondence regarding singers to be engaged for the event, particularly, of course, singers with the vocal qualities required for each role. The vocal scores used for rehearsals of the chorus did not arrive until February, leaving just two months to learn new and challenging music. Nonetheless, after the performance on April 13—the exact anniversary of the adoption of the Society's Constitution in 1815—Parker expressed complete satisfaction in the chorus's work. Unfortunately, the press and officers of the Society were not so happy. Boston's leading critic, H. T. Parker, noted of *Morven* that, "It interests, it stirs, but it never thrills," a view he attributed entirely to the score and not the performance.

The financial state of the Society was parlous after the centennial. Fewer and fewer people seemed inclined to purchase tickets for a Sunday evening concert. Over the coming years, Society President Courtenay Guild would repeatedly moan about the change from the days of the past, when no other entertainment was to be had on Sunday evenings. Increasingly it was possible to stay at home and listen to music on the phonograph, and, by the 1920s, there was the additional attraction of radio, which had the advantage of being free once one had a listening set. Moreover, former

Bronze medal with images of Handel and Haydn on the front and the Society's logo on the back. The medals were sold for $1.00 as part of the H&H Centenary Festival in 1915.

CENTENARY

·1815·
·1915·

THE·HANDEL·
AND·HAYDN·
SOCIETY·OF
BOSTON

HELEN·CHASE·BUSH

Thompson Stone,
H&H conductor
1927–1959

audience members might increasingly choose to go for a Sunday drive in their new automobiles and end up far from the downtown environs of the concert hall.

There were additional complaints, from the likes of H. T. Parker, that the Society's chosen repertory was too old-fashioned. After a performance of *Elijah*, Parker mentioned the many eyes that rolled to the ceiling of Symphony Hall during the performance. "How many of those eyes were there in rapture, or were counting the four dead lights in the central sunburst of the ceiling?" He concluded with a view that few dared make at the time: "*Elijah* is hopelessly, awfully, irremediably mid-Victorian." Mollenhauer had accomplished wonders with the chorus at the beginning of his term, but he was increasingly worn out, and though he continued with other activities, he resigned from the directorship of the Handel and Haydn Society on June 1, 1927. He died barely six months later.

For the first time, in searching for a new director, the Society's Board looked within the ensemble itself. Thompson Stone had been a member since 1903, and an officer since 1918, when he was elected to the Board of Directors. He was thus a well-known figure whose musical qualities would have been demonstrated nearly throughout Mollenhauer's directorship. He had gone to Europe to study piano with Theodore Leschitizky and conducting with Karl Muck (twice the music director of the Boston Symphony, and one of the most highly regarded in that line).

OPPOSITE
Souvenir program book of the Centenary Concerts, April 1915. The series of four concerts opened with Verdi's Requiem, followed by *Morven and the Grail* by Horatio Parker and commissioned by the Society, an Artists' Night, and closed with Mendelssohn's *Elijah*.

Almost immediately, Stone undertook to enlarge the repertory, though still retaining the *Messiahs*, the *Creations*, the *Elijahs*, and the Verdi Requiems that had been so much the core of the ensemble's work. He put on a joint program of thematically related works, one by the Italian Ermanno Wolf-Ferrari (*New Life*) and one by the American Henry Hadley (*New Earth*). The chorus also worked with the recently hired music director of the Boston Symphony, Serge Koussevitzky, who engaged H&H to sing two performances of *Messiah* with the Symphony to benefit its Pension Fund; this arrangement allowed two full rehearsals with orchestra—one more than was normally possible—and two performances. The Society was paid by the Symphony with a fee equal to the previous year's profit from *Messiah* performances, and established a still closer connection with the Symphony at just the time that organization was starting a quarter-century's collaboration with one of its most significant music directors.

It was a challenging year for the chorus, especially because of the need to learn the two new pieces by Wolf-Ferrari and Hadley, which were found to require a considerable amount of rehearsal. But it gave signs to the world at large that creaky old H&H had something stirring. There was even some novelty in the annual *Messiah* tradition. In 1929, the usual *Messiah* was offered on December 22 (Arthur Fiedler, later named the first American conductor of the Boston Pops, played harpsichord for this performance). The following afternoon a more varied program was offered, in response to frequent requests from the public. It included the first two cantatas from Bach's *Christmas Oratorio*, a chorus by Chadwick ("This is the Month"—the first choral movement of his cantata *Noel*, which he had tried to get the Society to perform nearly twenty years earlier), music by Sweelinck, and excerpts from *Messiah*. Unfortunately, ticket sales were not such as to induce a repetition of this kind of program. Nonetheless, in April 1930, Stone rather daringly joined that old favorite, the Verdi Requiem, to the Boston premiere of Kodály's *Psalmus Hungaricus*.

One area in which the venerable Handel and Haydn Society still remained entirely unchanged was its gender restriction for membership. Women had won the vote in the United States at large, but they were still not able to join as regular members of the Society. They were, of course, in demand as participants, but they could not participate in choosing the leaders of the group.

A woman *composer* might be involved in the programs, however, as Amy Beach had been in the 1890s, and as Mabel Daniels (1877–1971) had at the end of the Great War (*Peace with a Sword*), and was to be twice more in the history of the Society (*Exultate Deo*, 1931; and *A Psalm of Praise*, 1954). She was the daughter of the longtime president of the Society, George F. Daniels, and a student of Chadwick's; she

The Handel & Haydn Society All-Wagner Program

WOTAN'S FAREWELL TO BRUNHILDE (from painting by Delitz)

RIENZI

PARSIFAL

LOHENGRIN

Flying Dutchman

TANNHAUSER

Gotterdammerung

MEISTERSINGER

WALKURE

BOSTON OPERA HOUSE

WEDNESDAY EVENING, APRIL 24, 1935

later went to Munich and became the first woman admitted to the score-reading class there, normally limited to composers. (Her 1905 memoir, *An American Girl in Munich: Impressions of a Music Student*, is very enlightening.) At about the same time, Anita Davis-Chase was hired to run the business office of the Society—an increasingly necessary position as the financially dark times of the Depression settled in.

Women were also in demand for occasional social events. One of the most widely reported of these was a lively Valentine's Day party thrown by the women in 1933, possibly in the hope that it would raise spirits depressed by the world's economic situation. Each man received at least one Valentine, while Thompson Stone and Society President Courtenay Guild were laden with dozens of them. For all the roles they played in the Society, women were formally thanked by vote of the membership at its annual meeting; the men would rise formally to express this gratitude—a sentiment that was invisible to the recipients, who were not allowed to be present!

The 125th anniversary of the Society arrived in 1940—a dark time for the world and increasingly for the United States, though it was still keeping apart from the conflicts in Europe and Asia, other than arranging "lend-lease" (a way of supporting the war efforts of soon-to-be allies without committing provocative acts of war). It was not a time for great festivity. Even less, once we were drawn into the conflict.

Of course, in the 1940s, it was mostly men who went away to war, though increasingly women found ways to take part, whether in uniform or on the home front.

Note written by Elizabeth Burt, H&H manager, on December 16, 1943: "[1]943–1944 When the world was at war house sold out nine days ahead"

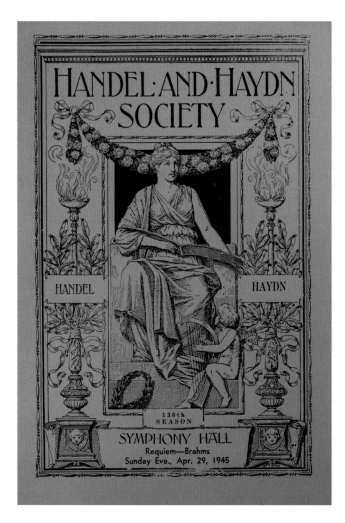

H&H performances continued with great difficulty, usually with the sponsorship of one organization or another. Perhaps the most memorable performance of that period was the Brahms' *German Requiem*—a work that, because of its difficult fugues, had not previously been heard in the Society's concerts. Stone gave careful preparation to the work, which was scheduled for April 29, 1945. Fate decreed, through the death of President Roosevelt, on April 12, that the performance should be dedicated to him, and to four members of the Society who had made the supreme sacrifice.

As the war came to an end, the Society felt the need for some degree of rejuvenation. Many of its leaders had been members for upwards of half a century, and there was again no mechanism by which those whose voices had ceased to contribute to the musical effect might be honorably retired. Stone was eager to start training younger voices, perhaps in a kind of training chorus to provide singers who might eventually graduate to the larger ensemble. He proposed re-auditioning everyone with more than twenty years of service. This alone reduced the older membership (presumably including a certain amount of dead wood) almost immediately. Not only did this

Program cover and insert for Brahms' Requiem concert, "In memory of President Franklin Delano Roosevelt, Late Commander-in-Chief, and to All the Members of Our Armed Forces who Have Made the Supreme Sacrifice," April 1945

Cover for H&H LP
recording of *Messiah*
on Unicorn Records,
issued in 1955

The Handel and Haydn Society of Boston presents

HANDEL'S

MESSIAH

conducted by Thompson Stone
with the Zimbler Sinfonietta

Adele Addison · soprano
Lorna Sydney · contralto
David Lloyd · tenor
Donald Gramm · bass

UNICORN RECORDS

THE CLASSICS RECORD LIBRARY

improve the musical quality of the chorus, it gave them a chance to compete with
newer choral groups with vigorous conductors arising in the Boston area.

One of Stone's last actions as conductor of the Society was to lead its first recording, of *Messiah*, issued by Boston-based Unicorn Records in 1955. This marked the
beginning of a new way in which the music and the performances might reach far
more widely than Boston—and that too would bring still more dramatic changes in
just a decade or so.

When Stone retired in 1959, the Board once again turned to the Society's own
membership to find its next music director and chose Dr. Edward F. Gilday, who
had conducted the Framingham Choral Society for the previous twenty years and
taught in colleges after earning a doctorate from Boston University. Once he took
command, Gilday wanted to move quickly to help the Society change its character
somewhat to better compete with the newer choruses in the Boston area.

Two points of Gilday's major plans for the ensemble may seem to be simple common sense: recruit more singers, especially younger singers with a stronger musical
training; and pay particular attention to public relations, recalling whenever feasible
the history of the organization and the role it had played for almost a century and
a half. Two other points of his plan are more forward-looking: take every opportunity to employ the mass media to spread the word about H&H—radio, television,
and recordings were all widespread realities in American life; and consider revising
the repertory to include a greater range of works—not just full-scale oratorios, but
smaller pieces, some without accompaniment, to provide a greater variety of sonority

OPPOSITE
Program for concert
on February 16, 1958.
A hand-written note
at bottom: "Cancelled
because of blizzard."

SOCIETY

HANDEL

HAYDN

143rd
SEASON

SYMPHONY HALL
SUNDAY EVENING
FEBRUARY 16TH 1958

CANCELLED BECAUSE OF
BLIZZARD

LEFT
Announcement for
the International
Choral Festival,
hosted by H&H
as part of its 150th
Anniversary

RIGHT
Program for
Inter-faith concert,
November 1964

international choral festival
handel and haydn society · 1815-1965

UNITED STATES
BRAZIL
NEW ZEALAND
JAPAN
GREAT BRITAIN
YUGOSLAVIA
CHILE
FINLAND
VENEZUELA
SOVIET UNION
HUNGARY
CANADA

150th anniversary celebration
symphony hall - jordan hall, boston · october 3-31, 1965

HANDEL AND HAYDN SOCIETY
DR. EDWARD GILDAY, Conductor

AN INTER-FAITH CONCERT
Symphony Hall
Sunday, November 1, 1964
3:30 p.m.

(and perhaps to save some of the expense of hiring a large orchestra for every program). And, finally, look to the coming sesquicentennial year of 1965.

During his time as music director of the Society, Gilday supervised the first national television broadcast of the complete, uncut *Messiah*, in December 1963, on WGBH. As had happened on several occasions in the past, the chorus was invited to take part in events of political or cultural significance, such as performing at an interfaith Roman Catholic/Protestant colloquium at Harvard University in March 1962. It also debuted as an opera chorus in *Boris Godunov*, produced by Sarah Caldwell's Opera Company of Boston in May 1965. As one of the special events of its 150th anniversary year, the Society hosted an international choral festival that brought fifteen choruses from eleven countries to Boston.

There was, however, one event of the 150th anniversary year that caused difficulties for Edward Gilday and, ultimately, led to his departure as music director of the Society. This resignation brought out the single most significant change in the Society's history.

Throughout the twentieth century—at first in small enclaves of performers and academics, then slowly moving into the mainstream—there was a growing number of performers who aimed to recover as much information as possible about how music was performed in previous eras. University programs offered classes in "performance

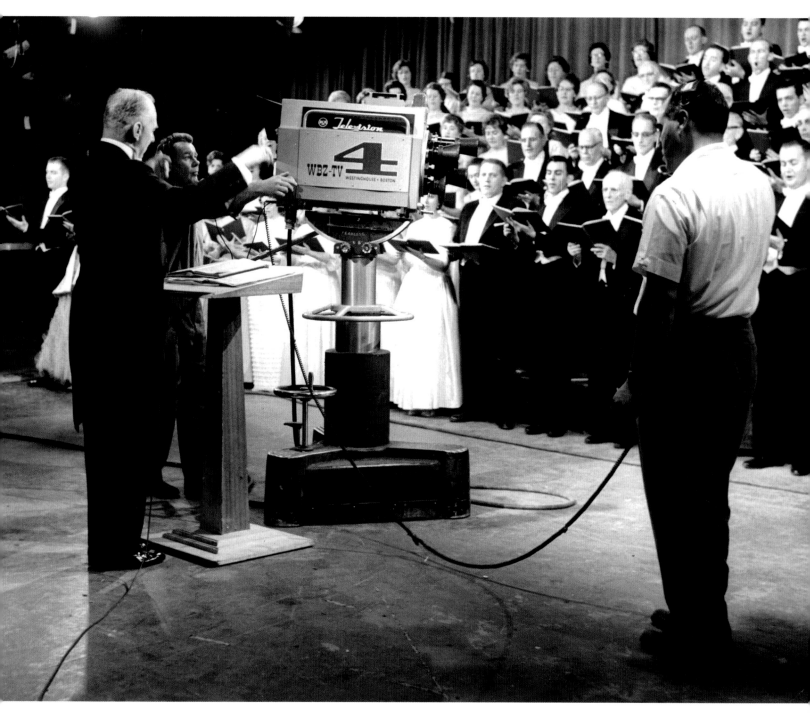

Edward Gilday conducting the H&H Chorus for *Accent on Music* on WBZ-TV, 1961

practice"—at first for graduate students, but eventually for students at every level, playing many kinds of instruments. Researchers pursued descriptions in old treatises on how to play the flute, or the violin, for example, to decipher how the musical notation was interpreted centuries before. Many musicians started playing both their modern instruments and early versions of the same instrument, which often had to be played quite differently and produced different sonorities.

This approach came to be called "HIP," short for "historically informed performance." For decades there was a growing divide between standard instrumental ensembles, playing recent music on modern instruments, and early music ensembles, playing older types of instruments in the ways they are thought to have been played when new.

The crisis at H&H erupted at roughly a mid-point of this development. Many performers had come to be interested in early performance styles, but still played them on their own traditional instruments. The crisis happened in connection with the concert that the Society always considered central to its existence: the annual *Messiah* performance.

In December 1965, Michael Steinberg, the new music critic of *The Boston Globe*, approached the task of reviewing that year's performance with a knowledge of the musicological literature of recent decades. His review lambasted almost every aspect of the performance, from the size of the chorus (gigantic, compared to what Handel had employed) and the orchestra (which represented an orchestration produced more than a century after Handel's death). Steinberg felt that H&H's tempos were heavy and inconsistent, the singers uneven.

Such goring of a sacred cow brought a flurry of responses, mostly vituperative attacks on Steinberg's perceptions—and almost all of those coming from listeners innocent of any connection with the recent developments in the understanding of Baroque performance. Steinberg offered space for a response from the Society's president, George E. Geyer, who suggested that Boston (or the Society) could "avoid your unduly severe criticisms" if they helped solve the problem of high performance costs, which allowed only a single orchestral rehearsal. Steinberg also referred to a performance in the "more original concept" the previous year in New York, under the direction of "one of America's most talented young choral-orchestral conductors," Thomas Dunn, though he noted that critical response considered it "not comparable to the full-throated versions of 'Messiah' that are part of our heritage and annual joy."

This debate in the letters pages of the *Globe* highlighted the divide between those who wanted to hear their Handel in the bloated, late-nineteenth-century style that

had become familiar, and those who found that smaller choruses and orchestras of comparable size offered a clearer view of Handel's counterpoint, presenting a more lithe and athletic character to the performance.

One letter came from Thomas Dunn himself, who pointed out that calls for a much smaller chorus ("twenty capable artists") had been made as early as 1891, by Bernard Shaw, and to follow that plan would provide an orchestra of modest size and allow more rehearsals at lower cost than the one employed by the Society in 1965. Dunn added, "I wonder if these questions will still be debated in the year 2039?"

The answer to his question is: no. America's oldest and most renowned choral organization for amateurs was about to become fully professional. In the process, it would also become a leading participant in the ongoing debate over historically informed performance.

H&H chorus and orchestra performing at Symphony Hall, 1963

PAGES 172–173
Two letters, dated 1929 and 1934, from conductor Thompson Stone to the H&H chorus, welcoming them back for a new season of singing and outlining his assessment of the previous season

TO THE MEMBERS OF THE CHORUS OF THE HANDEL & HAYDN SOCIETY:

Dear People:——

    Through the kindness of our President, Mr. Courtenay Guild,
I am enabled to write you this note of greeting before the opening
of our new season. I hope you have had a fine happy summer, and
that we shall have a finer, happier winter together.

    I did considerable thinking and work for the Society this
summer, which I hope will result in keener enjoyment for you at
the rehearsals and concerts, and added distinction to the Handel
& Haydn performances.

    Let me tell you now how delighted I was with your performance
of MESSIAH in June. It is the first time you have sung
MESSIAH to suit me. Now that you have found out how it is done,
please do not forget. I wish you could have heard the comments
from a great many of our audience, who packed the corridor and
green room back of the stage to say the most flattering things
about your singing. It was a truly great concert.

    This next season brings to us two a capella numbers for the
Christmas concert, in addition to the CHRISTMAS ORATORIO, the
MESSIAH, the Verdi REQUIEM, and the PSALMUS HUNGARICUS by Kodaly.
Here are old friends, and new acquaintances to be made. I am
especially eager to hear you sing the unaccompanied numbers, and
the great "Glory to God in the Highest" chorus from the CHRISTMAS
ORATORIO, and can hardly wait for the time when we shall be together
again.

    October 6th is our first rehearsal. I shall arrive at the
Hall at 5 o'clock in order to have a half hour to greet you before
the rehearsal commences at 5:30 sharp. The chorus seems to like the
custom I have inaugurated of singing the Hallelujah Chorus the
first thing at our first rehearsal. I hope you can arrange to be
in your place ready to sing this great chorus at the opening of
the rehearsal.

    Let me add a personal word of appreciation to the many members
of the chorus for their kindly spirit and generosity toward me
in many ways.

                                Sincerely,

                                THOMPSON STONE

P.S. The Hallelujah Chorus starts at 5:30!

Boston, Massachusetts
25 September 1929

29 OCTOBER, 1934

To My Friends, the Choristers of the Handel and Haydn Society:

The friendliest of greetings! I hope for the pleasure of making this greeting personal in the half hour before our first rehearsal—this coming Sunday, October 7th, at 5:30, in Huntington Hall. On the dot, at 5:30, we shall all stand and begin the season with the famous "Hallelujah." I, for one, can hardly wait.

At this rehearsal we shall rehearse some "new" music by Bach. That is, the Society has not sung it for many years. It will be new to most of you, and it is wondrous fine. Also new carols, and old, are to be rehearsed shortly for this year's carol concert. The carols were popular last year. My friend, "G. P.," told me last year he would bring fifteen people if we would give a similar concert this season. I shall hold him to it. Do your friends have the same feeling about attending our carols?

The singer has a special task. He must have a message to deliver, voice to convey the message, and a technique to express. So-o-o-o, begin to vocalize. How's the breath? Does the voice sound well? Can you "make it behave"? Practice—*every day.*

The training and experience of the past two years in particular is beginning to bear fruit. Your singing this last season not only brought joy to my heart, but pleasure to hundreds of others. Now, this year, a big step forward—in every way. I want to do things that will be of untold value to our old Society. Won't you help me? Working together, we will make the music into poetry, the poetry into music, and both of them into the finest vocal expression of human emotion, thought and inspiration.

President Guild, the Board of Government, Mr. Burbank and I will be at the head of the stairs Sunday next from 5:00 to 5:25 to say "hello" and chat with you. Come early—and be sociable.

Faithfully yours,

THOMPSON STONE

DONALD TEETERS

THE THOMAS DUNN ERA: 1967–1986

I N THE FALL of 1967, two venerable Boston institutions were again springing to life after long periods of drought, flaunting their newfound vigor in the face of all that was going on around them in the nation and the world. That year at Fenway Park, the Red Sox, coming from nowhere, astounded the sports world and countless Bostonians by coming within one game of winning it all in the World Series, an achievement that had eluded them since 1918.

Just across Back Bay, the even-more-venerable Handel and Haydn Society threw off the last vestiges of its nineteenth-century glories to embark on a startling new era of musical adventure. Amidst worldly turmoil, unpopular wars, assassinations, campus riots, and political opportunism, it was also, as it turned out, a time for radical reinvention in one of the Boston arts world's more sedate corners.

Thomas Dunn, whose appointment as H&H music director was announced in April 1967, had in the previous decade risen to high prominence in New York through his work as founding conductor of the Festival Orchestra of New York and of the (New York) Cantata Singers.

Born in 1925, in South Dakota, Dunn was reared in Baltimore. At age eleven he became assistant organist at a Baltimore church and, while still in high school, was named organist and, later, director of a professional choir in another church there. He received his bachelor's degree from Peabody Conservatory, where he studied with organists Virgil Fox and E. Power Biggs, and earned a master's degree from Harvard University in 1948, followed by studies at the Amsterdam Conservatory. In 1957, he was appointed music director at Madison Avenue's Church of the Incarnation, in New York, followed two years later by his appointment as leader of the Cantata Singers. The latter group had been conducted for many years by musicologist and Bach authority Arthur Mendel, who was a major force, along with Alfred Mann, in the

OPPOSITE
Thomas Dunn,
H&H conductor
1967–1986

emerging early music movement in this country. Mendel's work in Bach studies was a major influence on Dunn.

In both of his New York conducting posts, Dunn led an increasingly popular and critically praised series of early music performances that were worlds away from what most musicians and audiences had experienced before. In part, these were characterized by the use of smaller vocal and instrumental forces, an opening of textures through more and more varied articulations, and greater distinctions in dynamics and, especially, in the linear, i.e., contrapuntal elements—the interplay between two or more lines of music. The August 9, 1963, edition of *Time* magazine recognized Dunn's emerging influence in the early music movement, describing him as a "hero of the baroqueniks." The magazine called attention to three sellout performances earlier that season of all six of Bach's Brandenburg Concertos, and to Dunn's then-current Philharmonic Hall Midsummer Festival, which included a Mozart opera, major works by Handel, Bach's Mass in B Minor, and Stravinsky's *Symphony of Psalms*.

These performances reflected stylistic qualities and programming ideas that Dunn promised to bring to a rejuvenated Handel and Haydn Society in Boston. They would also signal a major change from past practices. Attractive, though less widely acknowledged, was the other hat that Dunn proudly wore: discoverer and reviver of works—both old and recent—that had, for whatever reasons, fallen off the radar screens of modern performing groups.

The circumstances, both internal and external, that prompted H&H to make a fundamental change in artistic direction and leadership can be traced to the December 1965 performance of Handel's *Messiah*. That performance of the oratorio prompted a period of shock, retrospection, and analysis by all those connected to the Society.

The performance was reviewed by, among others, *The Boston Globe's* music critic, Michael Steinberg, who, from 1964, had covered all aspects of the classical music scene in Boston. He was a force—many would say for good, though some, who bore the brunt of his printed tongue lashings, might disagree. His opinions were uncompromising and his influence pervasive in the community. He found fault with Boston Symphony performances so often that the players at one point voted to ban him from their concerts. Not surprisingly, management never put that ban into effect. In fact, Steinberg, after leaving the *Globe*, became the orchestra's program annotator.

Clearly, many aspects of that 1965 *Messiah* performance were thought by Steinberg to be unacceptable in a city of Boston's musical stature. In a number of citations he enumerated the failings: the stylistic inadequacies overall; the tempi, too slow, except for the movements that went too fast; "amazing retards in the middle of movements;" even the spelling of Handel's middle name, "Frederick," as the program book

Rehearsal at Symphony Hall

handel and haydn society

Thomas Dunn, music director

158th season

based on his Bach performances there. Not until March 1972, at the end of Dunn's fifth season, would H&H audiences first hear the monumental *St. Matthew Passion* under his leadership. And though, by 1972, the chorus size for *Messiah* and other pre-nineteenth-century works had been reduced, Dunn brought a full, eighty-five-voice chorus—still the all-volunteer, amateur chorus—to bear on this massive double-chorus, double-orchestra work; this was almost twice as many singers as the professionals he had employed in New York. His rationale: a group of amateur singers, properly rehearsed and singing with good discipline, could create textures as clean as a smaller group of professionals, and could be made to meet his needs and the work's requirements. It had taken five seasons for Dunn to train the H&H chorus to that level. Again, as in New York, the response to Dunn's concept and execution, indeed to all aspects of the performance, was a mix of stunned revelation and awe.

As can be seen in the detailed listing above of the works Dunn conducted in his early seasons in Boston, he was truly a musical omnivore. Combining scholarship, natural curiosity, and, yes, some degree of showmanship, he led his audiences into a trove of neglected old and recent works, sometimes brand new ones, too—including some commissioned by H&H on his recommendation—that he felt serious concertgoers had the right, indeed the obligation, to hear. Some of those works also involved dancers, some actors. His commitment to exploring a wide range of music in performances of great integrity marked Dunn's career in Boston as it had in New York, although the extent to which it included works outside the Baroque period surprised many in Boston who had been aware only of his reputation as a specialist in that field.

It is sad to report that, as Dunn approached the decadal anniversary of his arrival, the artistic achievements and substantial growth in audiences, which had been so widely heralded, were accompanied by serious internal frictions within the H&H Board, mainly having to do with finances. The principle item of contention was the large number and amounts of annual endowment reductions which had been made to cover budget deficits. As an institution, the Society had lived safely and conservatively for many years, realizing only the normal levels of income the endowment provided. But that safety came at a price. The organization had lost its will, not to say its ability to raise money.

Considering the new level of activity that Maestro Dunn brought with him—indeed was asked to bring with him—it should have been obvious that substantial fundraising would be essential, with the endowment available only as backup. It seems that the Board was just ill-equipped to meet the fundraising challenges, and the professional management in those days seems to have been similarly ill-equipped, or not properly challenged. So, by the mid-1970s, with the endowment only a remnant

OPPOSITE
Program cover for
April 27, 1973 concert
at Jordan Hall, which
included works by
Johannes Brahms,
Richard Felciano, and
the world premiere
of the revised version
of Daniel Pinkham's
Daniel in the Lion's Den.

Program cover for *Messiah*, December 1973

of its previous state, artistic goals and standards came into direct confrontation with financial realities. The Board minutes record extensive and hotly argued competing views to resolve the problem.

At the annual meeting in 1977, some of the officers expressed the view that the only solution was to substantially reduce the number of concerts, with a corresponding reduction in associated production and artistic costs. A competing group, supporters of Dunn's leadership, expressed equally strong views to the contrary. Dunn reminded the Board of its traditional responsibilities, among which was its fiduciary responsibility to see that adequate funds were raised to cover operating deficits. At this meeting, and on the spot, an opposing slate of officers was presented and voted in, an almost unprecedented action in the Society's history. These mostly younger, committed persons brought with them the determination to solve the financial problems in conformity with the then-current mission goals. And mostly they succeeded, beginning immediately to turn things around. Thus, after some uncomfortable verbal exchanges and soul-wrenching confrontations, the aged but newly revitalized institution lived to see another day.

Thomas Dunn and Max Miller, chair of the AGO Conference, "Inspecting the Gilmore Baton prior to its use in the H&H Society program for the American Guild of Organists Conference, June 1976."

At about this same time, the Handel and Haydn Society began the journey of evolving from an amateur choral society to one that would eventually become entirely professional, joining as equals chorus singers and their colleagues in the orchestra. Dunn had been looking forward to this for some time, even from his first season. At a Board meeting in April 1974, there was general discussion of, and subsequent agreement to, the "possibility of a reduction in the size of the chorus and a reduction in the number of programs," reportedly "causing some depression to current volunteer members of the chorus." But then, from the minutes of a Board of Governors meeting in September 1976, there was substantial agreement that "moves towards professionalism in all areas should be encouraged and implemented," although this did not mean "elimination of performances by the Society's large amateur chorus." It was not until March 1980 that the Board voted to establish a professional chorus, supported by a grant of $20,000 from the choral division of the National Endowment for the Arts.

Through the early 1980s, concert activity increased markedly. By the 1980–1981 season, H&H was booking seven concerts in its Symphony Hall series. Even though the endowment by this time was virtually exhausted, contributions from other sources had blossomed, including the National Endowment for the Arts, the Massachusetts Council for the Arts, the state's Arts Lottery, and private individual, foundation, and corporate giving.

Along with his commitment to diverse programming, Dunn was extraordinarily careful in his choice of soloists. Some had national reputations, such as the tenor Charles Bressler, and those mentioned above: Eunice Alberts, Hugues Cuénod, and

George Frideric Handel, Composer

MESSIAH

Chorus & Orchestra of the Handel & Haydn Society
Thomas Dunn, Conductor

STEREO S A 2015/8

Soloists:
Diana Hoagland
Barbara Wallace
Pamela Gore
George Livings
David Evitts

SINE QUA NON

SUPERBA

Cover for *Messiah* recording, 1977

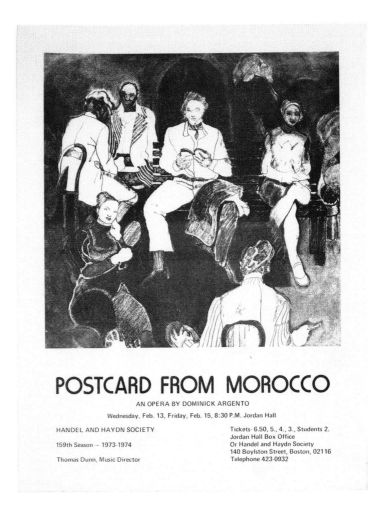

POSTCARD FROM MOROCCO

AN OPERA BY DOMINICK ARGENTO

Wednesday, Feb. 13, Friday, Feb. 15, 8:30 P.M. Jordan Hall

HANDEL AND HAYDN SOCIETY

159th Season – 1973-1974

Thomas Dunn, Music Director

Tickets· 6.50, 5., 4., 3., Students 2.
Jordan Hall Box Office
Or Handel and Haydn Society
140 Boylston Street, Boston, 02116
Telephone 423-0932

Richard Shadley. But he also gave significant, sometimes career-opening opportunities to singers who were based in or near Boston, among them, sopranos Barbara Wallace (a favorite singer in Dunn's early years in Boston; he also presented her in her New York debut as soloist in Handel's *Alexander's Feast*), Diana Hoagland, and Elizabeth Parcells; mezzo-soprano Jan Curtis (Dido in Dunn's presentation of the Purcell opera); altos Mary Davenport (an established artist who had made Boston her home) and Pamela Gore; tenor Jon Humphrey; and basses Sanford Sylvan, David Evitts, David Arnold, Francis Hester, and others—a distinguished company. Among the non-Bostonian soloists, New York soprano Jeanne Ommerle was singled out by the *Globe's* Richard Dyer as "the most ravishing Angel who ever bore glad tidings of great joy in *Messiah*."

Those who remember the period of Dunn's leadership at H&H will all have their own lists of memorable performances, but surely that list would include the two Bach Passions and the Mass in B Minor; the two great Haydn oratorios, *The Creation* and *The Seasons*; and that composer's several masses and less well-known *Il Ritorno di Tobia*. Other notable Dunn performances include, in a somewhat random listing,

H&H Chorus performing at Symphony Hall, 2010

H&H Chorus performing at Symphony Hall, 2012

H&H chamber music performance at Old West Church, 1989   Christopher Krueger, flute and Stephen Hammer, oboe

The rediscovery of music of the past has been going on for a long time. Ever since the museum culture of the nineteenth century, when cultural artifacts from the past began to be assembled for interpretation and enjoyment, artists, too, have sought to collect art, literature, drama, and music from past ages. In music this has meant the re-valuation of music of the Middle Ages, Renaissance, and Baroque—all those eras that seemed antiquated and outdated in an age that valued symphonies, Wagnerian and Verdian operas, and string quartets. The rediscovery of Gregorian chant, of Renaissance motets and madrigals, and of Baroque concerti and operas were aspects of this delight in taking seriously music that at one time had been discarded as outmoded.

Taking the music seriously, it follows, means serious performance. You can get great results when a string quartet plays a Palestrina motet, or when a big Steinway plays a Scarlatti sonata, but there are cases in which old music in modern performance arguably loses some of its magic. The Early Music "movement" takes the position that there was an interruption in the musical tradition; that somehow, at the French Revolution or about that time, there came a break. Nineteenth-century conservatories, like those in Paris and Leipzig, were created to train musicians for orchestral careers and as soloists for concerto and opera; tradition was handed on from teacher to pupil, and a uniform style of performance at a very high level was dominant for all styles of music then current. That performance style, featuring as it does continuous legato and vibrato, with a premium on the ability to project, to play and sing loudly (as concert halls and opera houses grew larger), is still with us today in our concert halls and opera houses. But it is arguably not the tradition that best suits the music of the eighteenth century and earlier. It is that earlier tradition—or those earlier traditions—that is meant by historically informed performance.

Andrew Schwartz, bassoon

Jesse Levine, trumpet

Curiosity bred research and experimentation. The differences between Baroque and modern stringed instruments and their performance were explored and refined; older instruments, like the harpsichord, the recorder, and the viola da gamba, were studied, restored, and renewed by instrument-makers. And the music that had seemed perhaps simple and antiquated rapidly became, in the hands of those who let the instruments do the explaining, a music of rare refinement and elegance, of dancing rhythms and passionate gestures.

Boston was in the forefront of these activities in the 1970s, but efforts had begun long before. Arnold Dolmetsch, the pioneering English maker of old instruments, spent the years 1905 through 1911 in Boston working for the Chickering Piano Company, where he made harpsichords, clavichords, and other hybrid instruments then in fashion. William Dowd and Frank Hubbard, first together, beginning in the late 1940s, and then separately, began building harpsichords along historical lines; the organ-builders Charles Fisk and Fritz Noack began creating period instruments in the 1960s; Friedrich von Huene crafted beautiful recorders and flutes; and other area makers fashioned lutes, violas da gamba, and a variety of other historical instruments.

Beginning in 1942, musicologist Erwin Bodky organized concerts of old music in the Houghton Library at Harvard University, played by members of the Boston Symphony Orchestra. Renamed the Cambridge Society for Early Music, the concert series continued in Sanders Theatre, often featuring international early music artists of the first rank; the Cambridge Society continues to this day. At the Museum of Fine Arts, Boston, the Boston Camerata presented concerts of early music that featured instruments from the Museum's impressive collection; independent after 1968, the group was directed until 2008 by Joel Cohen, and it continues under the direction of

Anne Azéma. Martin Pearlman's Banchetto Musicale, later renamed Boston Baroque, began small and grew in size and ability into a first-rate period ensemble.

OPPOSITE
Christopher Hogwood

The Boston Early Music Festival, initiated by many of Boston's leading performers and instrument-makers, began in 1981. It continues as a biennial festival and exhibition, centered around an operatic performance and including many official and fringe concerts, lectures, exhibitions, and workshops, generally attracting a large and varied audience of enthusiasts.

Boston is a center of education, and for decades the local institutions of higher learning have been engaged with research and training in early music. The composer and harpsichordist Daniel Pinkham for many years directed the early-music program at the New England Conservatory of Music; other such performance programs continue at Boston University and the Longy School of Music. Harvard University has hosted, in various capacities, many of the leading performers of early music, including August Wenzinger, Gustav Leonhardt, Frans Brüggen, and others, as well as being the academic home of the Bach scholar Christoph Wolff.

The Hogwood era at the Handel and Haydn Society was a step into the modern era of period instruments, but it was also, in a sense, the completion of a process begun some years earlier. Thomas Dunn's concern with artistic level and the professionalization of the chorus and the orchestra had gone a long way towards a future that neither he nor anybody else could see completely.

Judge Rya Zobel, who chaired the search committee that recommended Christopher Hogwood as artistic director, recalls that the committee, as such committees do, hoped to find a music director of superb musicianship, name recognition, and potential to increase the Society's public visibility and artistic standards. It did not set as its goal the conversion of the Society into a period-instrument orchestra and chorus. On the contrary, it was the vivid discussions of the committee with Christopher Hogwood as a candidate that convinced them, and then the governors, that Hogwood was their candidate, and that his vision was their vision. He thought they should concentrate on something more focused, and felt that early music and period instruments was the right direction and that the moment was now. "The choice of Chris," says Judge Zobel, "was a decision to focus and to go in a new direction."

Hogwood started off with a bang, announcing that the era of big-band historical performance had come to Boston. A splendid Mozart weekend, centered around the Requiem, but with lots more, was followed by H&H's first period-instrument *Messiah* and a spring full of Bach, Handel, Mozart, a big Purcell weekend, and a grand Haydn concert. Hogwood's London-based Academy of Ancient Music had made the first period-instrument recording of *Messiah*. He was well known for his clear and

incisive performances of Baroque music—music that was often already familiar as to its notes, but completely new to listeners who had never heard the sports-car version of beloved classics they thought were limousines.

Hogwood, in Boston, continued to produce Baroque greats, but a number of interesting explorations made the Society worth watching and listening to. It included nineteenth-century orchestral music (Early Music encroaching on the turf of Real Music!): Mendelssohn, Rossini, Spohr—all of whom had been performed by the Society in the nineteenth century. There was a splendid collaboration with the Mark Morris Dance Group in a production of Gluck's *Orfeo ed Euridice,* which toured to the Edinburgh Festival and elsewhere. There was the wonderful concert of H&H and the Dave Brubeck Ensemble, in which Hogwood's Bach alternated with Brubeck's Brubeck. The latter became a tradition. A similar concert, in 1999, featured Chick Corea and Gary Burton; in 2001, it was the Marian McPartland Trio; in 2003, the Dizzy Gillespie Alumni All-Stars; and in 2005, vibraphonist Gary Burton and pianist Makoto Ozone. And 1999 saw the world premiere of Dan Welcher's *JFK: The Voice of Peace*, narrated by David McCullough, which had been commissioned by the Society. The last season of the millennium closed, in April 2000, with a splendid three-day marathon of Vivaldi concerti.

Distinguished visiting conductors gave the Society, and Boston, a chance to experience the artistry of some wonderful leaders in the field of early music and of more standard repertoire; guests included Bernard Labadie, Andrew Parrott, William Christie, Ivor Bolton, Paul McCreesh, Harry Bicket, Grant Llewellyn, Robert Spano, Daniel Beckwith, Julian Wachner, and Rinaldo Alessandrini.

During all this time, the estimable John Finney, chorus master, keyboard virtuoso, and imaginative conductor, led performances of great interest, often a Christmas concert in Jordan Hall or a chamber concert of smaller dimensions but wider imagination than the larger works presented in the same season. These musical events provided a depth and variety that showcased the Society in all its aspects.

Michael Chance, Mark Morris, Christopher Hogwood. H&H collaborated with the Mark Morris Dance Group on a production of Gluck's *Orfeo*, 1996

With the millennium came a momentous transition: Christopher Hogwood's fifteen-year tenure as artistic director was celebrated with a splendid performance of Mendelssohn's *Elijah* and with a live broadcast of music by Mozart and Haydn on NPR's *SymphonyCast*, on April 22, 2001. In July, Grant Llewellyn became the new H&H music director and Christopher Hogwood was named conductor laureate.

It had been a wonderful fifteen years. Boston heard Handel operas (*Giulio Cesare, Semele, Acis and Galatea,* and, later, *Ariodante*), Mozart, Purcell. The Society developed a period orchestra of first-rate musicians, refined its already superb chorus, and presented to Boston in its concerts, and to the world in its tours and recordings, evidence that the Handel and Haydn Society was finely tuned, full of energy, and ready for more. There is much reason to be grateful to Christopher Hogwood.

Grant Llewellyn was a Welshman who at one point in his life had had to make the difficult choice between a career as a professional musician and one as a professional soccer player. Soccer's loss was Handel and Haydn's gain. The Llewellyn years can be characterized by an expansion of the repertory to include a substantial amount of nineteenth-century music using period concepts, and by a number of interesting projects combining older music and newer presentations. It started, suitably enough, with Handel and Haydn: first, Haydn's *Creation*, signaling a new beginning; and then *Messiah*, promising tradition and continuity.

In January 2002, members of the orchestra traveled to San Francisco to perform with Chanticleer, the acclaimed vocal ensemble, in the world premiere of John Tavener's *Lamentations and Praises*, co-commissioned by the Society, Chanticleer, and The Metropolitan Museum of Art. Performances were also given in Boston and New York City. The subsequent recording of the work garnered two Grammy awards.

A number of projects were undertaken in collaboration with the Chinese-born stage director Chen Shi-Zheng. Chen studied at the Hunan Art School in Traditional Opera and received his master's from the Tisch School of the Arts at New York University. His production of the twenty-hour Ming Dynasty opera, *The Peony Pavilion*, commissioned by the Lincoln Center Festival, premiered in New York in 1999. With Handel and Haydn, Chen staged the Monteverdi *Vespers of the Blessed Virgin Mary*, with hundreds of little Madonna statues, at the Cutler Majestic Theatre in 2003; later collaborations, equally inventive and interesting, were Purcell's *Dido and Aeneas*, in 2005, and Monteverdi's *L'Orfeo*, in 2006.

Many wondered how long it would be before Llewellyn took on the Ninth Symphony. It was not long: April 2003, on a program with Schoenberg's *Friede auf Erden.* Two pieces with important messages: Beethoven's "All are brothers" and Schoenberg's "Peace on earth." (I urged Llewellyn to place the chorus in front of the

OPPOSITE
Program for Dan Welcher's *JFK: The Voice of Peace*, March 1999. This concert marked the Youth Chorus' debut at Symphony Hall.

HANDEL & HAYDN SOCIETY

*America's Premier Chorus
and Period Orchestra*

Christopher Hogwood, Artistic Director

1998-1999 SEASON

CELEBRATING THE VOICE OF PEACE

Daniel Beckwith
CONDUCTOR

David McCullough
NARRATOR

Paul Tobias
CELLO

Handel & Haydn Society
Orchestra and Chorus

Handel & Haydn Society
Youth Chorus

MARCH 19 & 21, 1999
SYMPHONY HALL, BOSTON

Monteverdi's *Vespers of the Blessed Virgin Mary*, Cutler Majestic Theatre, Boston, 2003

Monteverdi's *L'Orfeo*, The Shubert Theatre, Boston, 2006

Purcell's *Dido and Aeneas*, Cutler Majestic Theatre, Boston, 2005

Purcell's *Dido and Aeneas*, Cutler Majestic Theatre, Boston, 2005

orchestra, as was always done in Beethoven's Vienna for concerts with orchestra and chorus; I have always wanted to hear what that sounds like. Grant told me that he tried it in a rehearsal but that he didn't think the sound was suitable. So the Ninth in Symphony Hall was arranged the way the Boston Symphony Orchestra and everybody else does it: orchestra in the front.)

There would be quite a lot more Beethoven: the "Eroica" Symphony and the "Emperor" Concerto in 2004; the First, Second, and Fifth Symphonies and the Violin Concerto in 2006. In a way it was a perfect match for Llewellyn: the period-instrument orchestra may have been teaching him something, but his Beethoven was really commanding, as was the more modern music: Brahms' *Haydn Variations* and Requiem, Verdi's *Four Sacred Pieces*. There were major works (Bach's B-Minor Mass, the *St. Matthew Passion*) and major soloists, but also wonderful concerts of music one doesn't hear very often: bits of Mozart, bits of Haydn, Baroque dances and concerti, opera arias by splendid soloists. Look through the seasons' programs and imagine what pleasures the audiences enjoyed.

Among many guest conductors of those years, Harry Christophers notably led the Society for the first time in 2006, at the Esterházy Palace, at a festival devoted to Haydn and Handel in Eisenstadt, Austria. Handel and Haydn plays Haydn and Handel in Haydn's own venue. This concert marked the Society's debut on the European continent and its first contact with its future leader.

In July 2006, Sir Roger Norrington was named artistic advisor of the Handel and Haydn Society. Grant Llewellyn took on the new role of principal conductor and Christopher Hogwood continued as conductor laureate. These moves recognized a shift in Llewellyn's ability to devote time to the Society owing to his growing commitments elsewhere. He had been a strong and regular presence on the scene for five years, making important contributions to the repertory and to the expansion of the repertorial horizons, especially with respect to later orchestral music.

Sir Roger Norrington first appeared with Handel and Haydn in 2007, leading Haydn's magnificent oratorio *The Seasons*. This was later brought to London's Royal Albert Hall for the BBC Proms, broadcast live throughout the United Kingdom on radio and television. The London *Telegraph* named it one of the top musical events of 2007. Sir Roger, somewhat like Christopher Hogwood, was by now a veteran, a sage, a guru of the early music world. He had created much of it and had seen it all, and now he was beginning to branch out in new directions: coming to H&H was part of this.

Norrington had been music director of the Kent Opera from 1969 to 1984. He founded the London Classical Players in 1978, with which he performed and

Grant Llewellyn

Sir Roger
Norrington and
H&H Board,
Symphony Hall,
2007

recorded widely. Elsewhere he sought to spread his knowledge, taste, and repertory to ensembles that were *not* period-instrument groups: he was principal conductor of the Bournemouth Sinfonietta from 1985 to 1989, and of the Stuttgart Radio Symphony Orchestra from 1998 to 2011; he directed the Orchestra of St. Luke's, in New York, from 1990 to 1994. Norrington's role at H&H was, at least partly, to stir things up. His conducting from memory, his wild turns to the audience at the ends of pieces ("How about that!" he seemed to say), his interesting programming, helped the Society maintain its traditions while injecting an additional ingredient into the mix. Sir Roger's involvement with the Society provided a creative transition to the current age, that of Harry Christophers.

Christophers, widely known for his skilled work in concerts and recordings with his chorus, The Sixteen, was appointed artistic director of the Society in 2008, and took up the position in earnest in 2009. He was steeped in the English choral tradition: he had been a member of the choirs of Canterbury Cathedral; Magdalen

OPPOSITE
Harry Christophers

College, Oxford; and Westminster Abbey; and sang professionally with The Clerkes of Oxenford and the BBC Singers. He knows his choral repertory. He has recorded widely with The Sixteen, and is in demand also to conduct opera. In 2012, he was made a Commander of the Order of the British Empire for his services to music.

Christophers' effort in Boston has been to refocus his, and the public's, attention on the Society's chorus, which has gone from strength to strength under his leadership. Highlights have been the Handel *Coronation Anthems*, the Mozart C-Minor Mass, a splendid *St. Matthew Passion*, a Handel *Jephtha* that toured to California—and *Messiah*, which Christophers has conducted with enthusiasm and to great acclaim each year since his arrival.

A survey of the 2007–2008 Season in a way provides a look at the Society over the last decades, and looks ahead to the Bicentennial celebrations. Concerts were led by Christopher Hogwood (Mozart and Haydn, with Boston Symphony Orchestra principal horn James Sommerville), Grant Llewellyn (Beethoven, Bach), Sir Roger Norrington (Haydn), and Harry Christophers (*Messiah*, Handel-Bach-Purcell)—the complete leadership roster of the Society's Historically Informed Performance era, with other concerts led by concertmaster Daniel Stepner, the invaluable John Finney, and Philip Pickett.

In February 2011, Christophers and the Society launched a Bicentennial series, performing masterworks it had premiered in America in the nineteenth century.

John Finney, H&H chorusmaster 1990–2014 and associate conductor 1992–2014

H&H teacher-in-residence
Jennifer Ashe at the Kennedy School
in Boston, November 18, 2013

The series began with performances of Handel's *Israel in Egypt*; this was followed by Bach's *St. Matthew Passion* in 2012, Handel's *Jephtha* in 2013, and Handel's *Samson* in 2014. As Judge Zobel remarked, "Each of the conductors"—she means Hogwood, Llewellyn, Norrington, and Christophers—"has brought something new and important to the Society; each served the Society beautifully at the right time, for the right length of time, and the changes were all good."

The Society has not only configured itself as a leading period-instrument orchestra and chorus, but has assumed an important role in developing an active participation in music among younger listeners and performers. This was a conscious effort of the governors, according to Robert Scott, president from 1992 to 2000: "The governors asked," he says, "'What can we do in schools to help people to discover music, and to help them discover whether they have any musical interest and ability?'" They found plenty to do. The Karen S. and George D. Levy Education Program, which now serves thousands of children throughout eastern New England, celebrates its 30th anniversary at the Society's Bicentennial. The Society's current endeavors are not so much part of a history as an ongoing effort to lead the Society into the future.

To give an idea of the scope of these activities: there is a Vocal Arts Program that provides instruction and performance opportunities through several choruses for young children through high-school-age students, under the leadership of superb musicians. These youth ensembles appear with H&H on the stage of Symphony Hall and in many other venues, and provide enormous pleasure to the participants and to their listeners. H&H's various educational programs bring people to music,

Performance at the Museum of Fine Arts, Boston, 2011

and they bring music to people. H&H has instituted programs of various kinds with local institutions, such as the Massachusetts Institute of Technology, the Massachusetts College of Art and Design, the New England Conservatory, the Boston Public Library, the Museum of Fine Arts, the Boston Children's Museum—the Society is clearly a concerned and contributing citizen in one of the world's most artistic cities.

At Harvard University, the Society premiered Robert Levin's reconstruction of a fragmentary horn concerto by Mozart. On a personal note, there was for some years, beginning in the Llewellyn era, a program that allowed the Society's orchestra to appear twice in Harvard's Sanders Theatre for my large undergraduate class called *First Nights*. On those occasions, the orchestra, conducted sometimes by Grant, sometimes by a guest, would explore with me one movement of Beethoven's Ninth Symphony or Berlioz's *Symphonie fantastique*. I spoke, Grant commented, and we played excerpts from the movement in question before playing the whole piece. This allowed students to hear things that one cannot hear in a single performance.

OPPOSITE
Performance at the African Meeting House, Boston, 2012

The educational activities of the Society, at all levels, contribute to making people feel that they are insiders, that they have almost a proprietary interest in the well-being of the music: an excellent way to prepare for the future.

In the nineteenth century, the planning, coordination, and implementation of any single season was managed by the H&H Board, which chose the repertoire, hired soloists and orchestra as needed, and oversaw all aspects of the Society. With H&H's expanding role in the twentieth century, particularly in education, a larger administrative base was needed.

In the period covered by this chapter, the increasing precision, focus, and solid foundation established by the musical efforts of the Society have been paralleled, and indeed made possible, by the imagination and abilities of an increasingly professional and dedicated administrative staff. After the departure of General Manager Deborah Borda, in 1979, a series of general managers, each serving a short time, preceded the arrival of Mary (Hall) Deissler, who led the Society as general manager and then as executive director for a quarter century, from 1982 through 2007. For twenty-five years, she shaped important institutional changes that brought complete professionalization to the Society, with strong fundraising and audience development initiatives and an eagerness to support innovative programs. She oversaw and enabled the many changes in the musical activities of the Society and worked to strengthen the staff and increase the Society's ability to serve its core mission of bringing great music to people.

One of Mary Deissler's favorite memories is of a viola player in the orchestra, Lorraine Hunt, who was singled out by Christopher Hogwood as his chosen vocal soloist for a concert version of Mozart's *La clemenza di Tito*. Deissler was surprised, since not every orchestral player can be expected to sing. But Hogwood was right, and Lorraine Hunt, known as Lorraine Hunt Lieberson after her marriage to the composer Peter Lieberson, went on to a brilliant vocal career.

Under the leadership of Deissler's successor, Marie-Hélène Bernard, the Society has strategically positioned itself as a platform for performers, patrons, and educators, to bring together a community that embraces live performances and impactful education and outreach programs accessible to all. The Society's dedicated efforts to developing a younger and more diverse audience and an impressive number of institutional and artistic partnerships came to cement the organization's standing as a leader in the field of early music and education programs. While more than doubling the size of its endowment as it approaches its 200th anniversary in 2015, H&H truly broadened its perspective from a local community organization to an H&H staff, 2014 international one.

TOP
Gala co-chairs, 2011:
Kathleen Weld, H&H
Board of Governors,
Alli Achtmeyer, and
Deborah First, H&H
Board of Governors

MIDDLE
Todd Estabrook, H&H
president, 2005–2010,
and John Tenhula

BOTTOM
Marie-Hélène Bernard,
Nicholas Gleysteen,
H&H chair, and Harry
Christophers

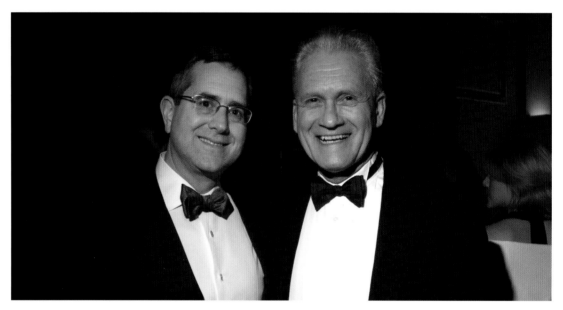

What is the future of the Society? What is the future of music in our world? Nobody can predict it. In a digital age in which all music is available all the time, and in which live music-making is at once more common than ever and in another sense rarer, what is the place of the Handel and Haydn Society? H&H Governor Robert Scott, who in 2013 marked the fiftieth anniversary of attending his first H&H *Messiah*, feels that the future is bright: "The Society has a solid foundation, a good plan, musical ideas, great leadership, and is increasingly able to appeal to people."

The Society, says Todd Estabrook, presents "music that speaks to the bottom of my soul, and we must present it to the next generation." Current Chairman Nicholas Gleysteen remarks that, in its recent history, the Society had explored broadly, and is now "focusing on what it does best, what its audience enjoys, and what will carry it with strength into the future."

Whatever that future may be, it will be a splendid one.

Harry Christophers, Marie-Hélène Bernard, and H&H Board, 2011

PAGES 226–227
H&H Period Instrument Orchestra and Chorus, taking their bows at Symphony Hall, 2013

ORATORIOS,

COMPRISING

THE MESSIAH......BY HANDEL,

AND

THE CREATION......BY HAYDN,

TOGETHER WITH

INTERMEDIATE SELECTIONS;

AS PERFORMED

AT KING'S CHAPEL, BOSTON,

ON THE

EVENINGS OF THE FIRST, THIRD, AND FOURTH APRIL, 1817,

BY THE

HANDEL AND HAYDN SOCIETY.

BOSTON:
PRINTED BY C. STEBBINS.
1817.

THE MESSIAH,

AN ORATORIO,

IN THREE PARTS;

AS PERFORMED AT BOYLSTON-HALL

BY THE

HANDEL AND HAYDN SOCIETY,

On Friday evening, (GOOD FRIDAY) March 31, 1820.

PART FIRST.

AIR.

Comfort ye my people, saith your God; speak ye comfortably to Jerusalem, and cry unto her, that her warfare is accomplished, that her iniquity is pardoned. The voice of him that crieth in the wilderness, Prepare ye the way of the Lord, make straight in the desert a highway for our God.

AIR.

Every valley shall be exalted, and every mountain and hill made low; the crooked straight, and the rough places plain.

CHORUS.

And the glory of the Lord shall be revealed, and all flesh shall see it together: for the mouth of the Lord hath spoken it.

RECITATIVE.

Thus saith the Lord, the Lord of hosts, Yet once a little while, and I will shake the heavens and the earth, the sea, and the dry land; and I will shake all nations; and the Desire of all nations shall come. The Lord, whom ye seek, shall suddenly come to his temple, even the Messenger of the covenant, whom ye delight in; behold he shall come, saith the Lord of hosts.

FORTY-SECOND SEASON.

HANDEL'S GRAND ORATORIO,

THE

MESSIAH,

WILL BE PERFORMED BY THE

Handel and Haydn Society,

AT THE

BOSTON MUSIC HALL,

ON SATURDAY EVENING, DEC. 26, 1857,

FOR THE POOR OF BOSTON, TO BE DISPENSED THROUGH THE

AGENCY OF THE

Boston Provident Association.

The following resident Vocalists have kindly volunteered their services:—

MRS. J. H. LONG, MRS. E. A. WENTWORTH,

MRS. T. H. EMMONS,

MR. C. R. ADAMS,

MR. J. Q. WETHERBEE.

CARL ZERRAHN....................Conductor.

J. C. D. PARKER......................Organist.

Tickets, at ONE DOLLAR each, with reserved seats, for sale at Messrs. Russell & Richardson's, 291 Washington Street.

Doors open at 6: Commence at 7 o'clock.

Balch, Printer, 21 School St.

FORTY-[...]

Handel and [...]

HAVING EFFECT[...]

THE ITALIAN [...]

WILL PERFORM [...]

THE M[...]

BOSTON [...]

EASTER SUNDAY [...]

WITH THE

Miss Clara L[...]
Miss Isabel[...]
Miss [...]

AND A FUL[...]

Sig. MUZIO AND CAR[...]

B. J. LANG, [...]

TICKETS, (with Reserv[...]

Doors open at 6½ [...]

Balch, Print[...]

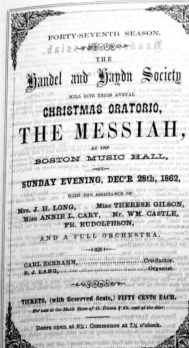

Handel and Haydn Society.

FORTY-SIXTH SEASON.

ORATORIO ON NEW YEAR'S DAY!

HANDEL'S MESSIAH

WILL BE REPEATED, AT THE

BOSTON MUSIC HALL,

ON

WEDNESDAY AFTERNOON, JAN. 1st, 1862,

FOR THE BENEFIT OF THE

U. S. SANITARY COMMISSION FUND.

SOLOISTS.

Mrs. J. H. LONG, Mrs. JENNY KEMPTON,

Miss GILSON, Mr. GUSTAVUS GEARY,

Mr. J. R. THOMAS,

AND A FULL ORCHESTRA.

CARL ZERRAHN.................Conductor.

B. J. LANG.........................Organist.

TICKETS, (with Reserved Seats,) FIFTY CENTS EACH.

For sale at the Music Store of O. Ditson & Co. and at the door.

Doors open at 2: Commence at 3 o'clock.

Balch, Printer, 34 School St., Boston.

FORTY-SEVENTH SEASON.

THE

Handel and Haydn Society

WILL GIVE THEIR ANNUAL

CHRISTMAS ORATORIO,

THE MESSIAH,

AT THE

BOSTON MUSIC HALL,

ON

SUNDAY EVENING, DEC'R 28th, 1862,

WITH THE ASSISTANCE OF

Mrs. J. H. LONG, Miss THERESE GILSON,

Miss ANNIE L. CARY, Mr. WM. CASTLE,

FR. RUDOLPHSON,

AND A FULL ORCHESTRA.

CARL ZERRAHN......................Conductor.

B. J. LANG.............................Organist.

TICKETS, (with Reserved Seats,) FIFTY CENTS EACH.

For sale at the Music Store of O. Ditson & Co. and at the door.

Doors open at 6½: Commence at 7½ o'clock.

Balch, Printer, 34 School St., Boston.

THE MESSIAH,

A SACRED ORATORIO,

BY HANDEL,

TO BE PERFORMED BY THE

HANDEL AND HAYDN SOCIETY,

Sunday Evening, Jan. 5th, 1840,

AT THE

MELODEON.

PART I.

OVERTURE.

RECITATIVE.   [Orch. No. 11.]

Comfort ye, comfort ye my people, saith your God; speak ye comfortably to Jerusalem, and cry unto her, that her warfare is accomplished, that her iniquity is pardoned.
The voice of him that crieth in the wilderness; prepare ye the way of the Lord, make straight in the desert a high way for our God.

AIR.

Every valley shall be exalted, and every mountain and hill made low; the crooked straight, and the rough places plain.

CHORUS.

And the glory of the Lord shall be revealed, and all flesh shall see it together; for the mouth of the Lord hath spoken it.

RECITATIVE.   [Orch. No. 12.]

Thus saith the Lord of Hosts: Yet once a little while, and I will shake the heavens and the earth, the sea and the dry land, and I will shake all nations; and the desire of all nations shall come; the Lord whom ye seek, shall suddenly come to his temple, even the messenger of the covenant whom ye delight in; behold he shall come, saith the Lord of Hosts.

CHORUS.   [Orch. No. 14.]

And he shall purify the sons of Levi, that they may offer unto the Lord an offering in righteousness.

RECITATIVE.   [Orch. No. 15.]

Behold a virgin shall conceive and bear a son, and shall call his name Emanuel;—God with us.

FIFTIE[...]

Handel and [...]

THE [...]

HA[...]

MES[...]

AS PER[...]

BOSTON [...]

On SUNDAY EVE[...]

MLLE. [...]
Miss ADELAIDE PHIL[...]
Mr. M. [...]

The Large Chorus of [...]

500 [...]

An increased Orches[...]

CARL ZERRAHN,.....[...]
B. J. LANG,.....[...]

TICKETS $2.00 and $1.5[...]

Doors open at 6½ [...]

Balch, Printer, [...]

Inaugurated 1815.

Handel and Haydn Society.

HANDEL'S ORATORIO

H. & H. SOC. ADMISS.

THE MESSIAH,

AS PERFORMED AT THE

Boston Music Hall,

ON

SUNDAY EV'G, DEC. 21, 1873.

PRINCIPAL VOCALISTS.

Mrs. H. M. SMITH.
Mrs. H. E. SAWYER.
Mr. NELSON VARLEY.
Mr. MYRON W. WHITNEY.

Full CHORUS of the SOCIETY, ORCHESTRA, and the GREAT ORGAN.

B. J. LANG, Organist.

CARL ZERRAHN, Conductor.

Tickets with secured seats, $1.50 and $1.00, according to location. The oratorio will commence at 7 o'clock precisely.

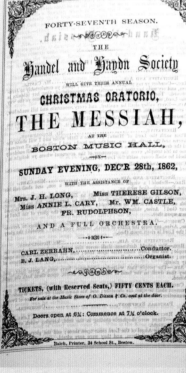

THE

ORATORIO

OF THE

MESSIAH

TO BE PERFORMED BY THE

HANDEL AND HAYDN SOCIETY,

AT THE MELODEON,

On Christmas Eve, Dec. 24, 1848,

ASSISTED BY

Miss ANNA STONE, | Miss PROVOST,

Mr. J. L. HATTON.

Mr. GEO. F. HAYTER.........Organist.

Mr. C. E. HORN...............Director.

Performance to commence at 7 o'clock.

BOSTON:
OAKES & SOLOMONS, No. 20 STATE STREET.
1848.

HANDEL AND HAYDN SOCIETY.

THE MESSIAH;

A SACRED ORATORIO:

Words Selected from the Holy Scriptures.

The Music Composed in the year 1741,

BY

GEORGE FREDERICK HANDEL.

PERFORMED BY THE SOCIETY

AT THE

BOSTON MUSIC HALL,

DECEMBER 24, 1854.

Boston:
PUBLISHED BY THE SOCIETY.

Holman, Gray & Co., Printers, N. Y.

HANDEL AND [...]

The [...]

WILL BE P[...]

HANDEL & H[...]

SUNDAY EVENING[...]

AT[...]

Boston M[...]

ASSISTED [...]

Miss ADELAIDE PHILLIPS,
Mrs. E. A. WENTWORTH,
Mr. S. [...]

CARL ZERRAHN,....CONDUCTOR.

Doors open at 6 o'clock.

TICKETS, FIFT[...]

May be had at the principal Music [...] and of H. L. HAZELTON, Secretary [...]

NOTICE.—The audience are respectfully and [...]

From J. S. Potter's Printing [...]

APPENDIX 1

H&H PREMIERES AND COMMISSIONS

When the Handel and Haydn Society was founded, in 1815, Handel represented the "old" in music and Haydn the "new." H&H has never forgotten its beginnings as an organization dedicated to this two-fold principle. The Society premiered many works in America and commissioned new ones throughout the nineteenth and early twentieth centuries. Even as the orchestra and chorus became dedicated to historically informed performance, the Education Program began commissioning new works, continuing a tradition begun nearly two hundred years earlier.

AMERICAN PREMIERES

Handel, *Messiah*, December 25, 1818

Haydn, *The Creation*, February 16, 1819

Mozart, Mass in C (possibly "Coronation" Mass or *Missa longa*), April 12, 1829

Handel, *Samson*, January 26, 1845

Beethoven, *Engedi*, February 6, 1853

Handel, *Solomon*, November 18, 1855

Handel, *Ode for St. Cecilia's Day*, November 28, 1863

Handel, *Jephtha*, February 17, 1867

Michael Costa, *Naaman*, March 26, 1869

J. S. Bach, *St. Matthew Passion* (selections), May 13, 1871

Handel, *Joshua*, April 16, 1876

Verdi, Requiem, May 5, 1878

J. S. Bach, *St. Matthew Passion* (complete), April 11, 1879

Karl Heinrich Graun, *Der Tod Jesu*, February 5, 1882

Max Bruch, *Arminius*, May 4, 1883

Théodore Dubois, *Paradise Lost*, February 8, 1903

Fritz Volbach, *Raphael*, February 19, 1905

Handel, *Belshazzar*, March 31, 1907

Marco Enrico Bossi, *Paradise Lost*, March 27, 1910

Pēteris Vasks, *Dona Nobis Pacem* (with H&H Youth Chorus), April 21, 2012

BOSTON PREMIERES

Charles E. Horn, *Remission of Sin*, October 2, 1836

Mendelssohn, *St. Paul*, January 22, 1843

Rossini, *Stabat Mater*, February 26, 1843

Handel, *Judas Maccabaeus*, December 5, 1847

Mendelssohn, *Elijah*, February 13, 1848

Donizetti, *The Martyrs*, December 16, 1849

Beethoven, Symphony No. 9, February 5, 1853

Mozart, Requiem, January 18, 1857

Michael Costa, *Eli*, February 15, 1857

Mendelssohn, *Hymn of Praise (Lobgesang)*, April 10, 1858

Handel, *Israel in Egypt*, February 13, 1859

Mendelssohn, *Christus*, May 7, 1874

John Knowles Paine, *St. Peter*, May 9, 1874

Haydn, *The Seasons*, April 28, 1875

B. Marcello, arranged by P. J. Lindpainter, *Psalm XVIII: "The Spacious Firmament,"* May 17, 1877

Saint-Saëns, *Oratorio de Noël*, op. 12, May 17, 1877

Ferdinand Hiller, *A Song of Victory*, May 17, 1877

J. C. D. Parker, *Redemption Hymn*, May 17, 1877

Cherubini, Mass in D Minor, May 2, 1883

Gounod, *Mors et Vita*, January 24, 1886

OPPOSITE
Messiah programs
from the 19th century

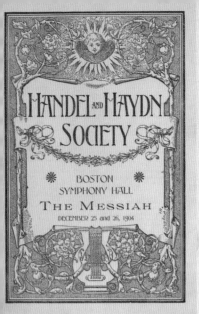

BOSTON PREMIERES (cont.)

J.S. Bach, Mass in B Minor (selections),
February 27, 1887

Berlioz, *Te Deum*, January 29, 1888

George W. Chadwick, *Phoenix expirans*,
February 5, 1893

Horatio Parker, *Hora Novissima*, February 4, 1894

John Knowles Paine, *Hymn of the West*,
February 19, 1905

Henry Hadley, *The New Earth*, April 8, 1928

Kodály, *Psalmus Hungaricus*, April 6, 1930

Mabel Daniels, *Exultate Deo*, April 5, 1931

W. F. Bach, *Lasset Uns Ablegen*, April 10, 1932

Karol Szymanowski, *Stabat Mater*, April 10, 1932

Heinrich Kaminski, *Magnificat*, April 10, 1932

Mabel Daniels, *The Holy Star*, December 20, 1934

Philipp Nicolai, arranged by Georg Schumann,
Wake, Arise, December 20, 1934

Verdi, *Quattro Pezzi Sacri*, April 3, 1966

Richard Felciano, *Glossolalia*, December 27, 1967

John LaMontaine, *Wonder Tidings*,
December 27, 1967

Honegger, *Le dit des jeux du monde*,
February 8, 1969

Rameau, *Les Incasa du Pérou*, October 10, 1969

Britten, *Nocturne, Op. 60*, March 6, 1970

Richard Felciano, *Background Music*,
February 29, 1971

Sweelinck, *Psaume CL*, October 29, 1971

Dominick Argento, *Postcard from Morocco*,
February 13, 1974

Haydn, *Il Ritorno di Tobia*, December 12, 1975

Conrad Susa, *Transformations*, March 26, 1976

Karl Jenkins, *The Armed Man: A Mass for Peace*,
April 20, 2008

WORLD PREMIERES

Charles Zeuner, *Grand Organ Concerto*, May 18, 1834

H.H.A. Beach, Mass, February 7, 1892

Mabel Daniels, *Peace With a Sword*, February 17, 1918

Daniel Pinkham, *Daniel in the Lion's Den*
(revised version), April 27, 1973

Dan Welcher, *JFK: The Voice of Peace* (with H&H
Youth Chorus and H&H Youth Soloists),
March 19, 1999

Tom Vignieri, *Hodie Christus natus est*,
December 3, 2005

Tom Vignieri, *Fanfare of Voices*, March 20, 2009

Silvio Amato, *Illuminescence: Prayers for Peace*
(H&H Young Men's and Young Women's
Choruses with the New England Conservatory
Philharmonic Youth Orchestra and Chorale
as part of the City of Boston's "Day of
Remembrance"), September 11, 2011